CRIME AND PUNISHMENT

Issues in Criminal Justice

CRIME AND PUNISHMENT

ISSUES IN

CRIMINAL JUSTICE

Edited by

FRED E. BAUMANN

KENNETH M. JENSEN

Published for the Public Affairs Conference Center
Kenyon College
by the University Press of Virginia
Charlottesville

THE UNIVERSITY PRESS OF VIRGINIA

Publication of this volume is sponsored by the Kenyon Public Affairs Conference Center, Kenyon College, Gambier, Ohio. The authors alone are responsible for the opinions expressed and any policies recommended in their respective papers. The Kenyon Public Affairs Conference Center is a nonpartisan educational program and as such takes no position on questions of public policy.

First published 1989

Library of Congress Cataloging-in-Publication Data
Crime and punishment : issues in criminal justice / edited by Fred E.
Baumann, Kenneth M. Jensen.
p. cm.
Includes index.
ISBN 0–8139–1191–5
1. Criminal justice, Administration of—United States—Congresses.
2. Punishment—United States—Congresses. I. Baumann, Fred E.
II. Jensen, Kenneth M. (Kenneth Martin), 1944– . III. Public
Affairs Conference Center.
HV9950.C743 1989
364′.973—dc19 88–25854
CIP

Printed in the United States of America

Contents

Preface
FRED E. BAUMANN
vii

Retribution as the Ground for Punishment
WALTER BERNS
1

Moral Science, Social Science, and the Idea of Justice
DANIEL N. ROBINSON
15

Reason, Anger, and Retribution
JEFFREY LEIGH SEDGWICK
41

Punishment and the Criminal Justice System: A Prosecutor's Viewpoint
WILLIAM J. KUNKLE, JR.
62

The Integrity of the Retributive Ideal
JEROME H. SKOLNICK
81

Beyond Rehabilitation
AUSTIN D. SARAT
103

Contributors
127

Author Index
129

Subject Index
131

Preface

"There is a point in the history of society," Friedrich Nietzsche predicted, "when it becomes so pathologically soft and tender that among other things it sides even with those who harm it, criminals, and does this quite seriously and honestly. Punishing somehow seems unfair to it, and it is certain that imagining 'punishment' and 'being supposed to punish' hurts it, arouses fear in it. 'Is it not enough to render him *undangerous*? Why still punish? Punishing itself is terrible.'"[1] Whatever heights of exasperation the current debate about crime and punishment may reach, the charge is rarely put quite so harshly or so apocalyptically. Yet, abstracting from what one may think of Nietzsche's own preferences in the matter, the fact that his words remain so shocking suggests that it is true enough that liberal democratic societies like ours have a particular problem with such weighty and weighted terms as "crime," "responsibility," and above all "punishment." Torn between a desire for domestic tranquility, which seems to require a vigilant police and an effective judiciary and penal system, and an increasing sensitivity not only to possible cases of injustice in punishment but even more to the inherent hurtfulness of punishment itself, societies like ours find themselves frequently casting about for a way to "render undangerous" without harming or committing counter-injustice. Yet, recent experience seems to show, finding such satisfactory ways is not so easy.

Twenty years ago a typical conference on this subject, while it might have contained a number of utilitarians who believed that the central purpose of criminal justice was to lower the crime rate and a scattering of retributivists who believed that above all there was a moral obligation to punish crime, would surely have given pride of place to rehabilitationists who believed that modern penology and psychology would soon enable us to "render undangerous" without depriving those so rendered of dignity and humanity. In 1983, when the Kenyon Public

Affairs Conference Center sponsored the conference out of which this volume emerged, the picture was quite strikingly different. Rehabilitationists were not to be found for love or for the money available, and predominating over a small group of utilitarians was a large and confident band of retributivists. Most strikingly, however, this did not coincide simply with fundamental changes in policy positions. The civil libertarians and those who wanted lighter sentencing were still civil libertarians and still wanted lighter sentences; now, however, they made retributivist arguments for their positions. And, as might be deduced, some pretty basic disagreements among the retributivists emerged as well.

One of the key arguments in the conference can be retraced in the papers of Walter Berns, Daniel Robinson, and Jeff Sedgwick. All three offer retributivist justifications for punishment, but Berns, following Aristotle, makes a case for the legitimacy of anger in punishment. By contrast, Robinson, in the Kantian tradition, argues for a retributivism whose great boast is that it can provide justice rationally and impartially but precisely without a deforming and unworthy anger. Sedgwick seeks to elucidate the principles underlying the conflict. In doing this, it seems to me, the three authors have done much to offer solid intellectual grounding to a newly revived movement in criminal justice policy.

The essays of William Kunkle and Jerome Skolnick can perhaps be thought of as coupled in some way. Kunkle, then a prosecuting attorney in Chicago, speaks urgently and graphically about the effort to control nearly uncontrollable crime. To me one of the most interesting parts of his essay concerns the prosecutor's own scale of what punishment certain crimes are "worth." If Kunkle can be thought to represent what the late Herbert Packer called the "Crime Control Model" of criminal justice, Skolnick can be identified as the representative of the alternative "Due Process Model." Taken together, these models and the tendencies underlying them depict the range in which debate normally takes place in the United States as we are torn between the desire to keep the peace and the desire to avoid all injustice.

Finally, the essay by Austin Sarat offers a valuable perspective on the state of the overall debate. Acknowledging the changed environment, he encourages us to think past the old quarrels and to see where the new tendencies might lead, especially in the area of sentencing. As moderator of the conference and editor of the book, it seemed to me that both suggested that there is considerable shifting of old positions and hence openness to new formulations in the current debate on criminal justice. This volume is meant to contribute to that debate and, I hope, to that openness.

Special thanks are due to the John M. Olin Foundation, which not only supported the publication of this book by a special grant but also gave support to the work of the PACC, as well as to all the other supporters of the PACC including the Sarah Scaife Foundation, Inc., the Procter & Gamble Fund, and Marathon Oil Foundation, Inc. I am most grateful as well to Sheryl Furniss, the PACC's able secretary; to Judy Sacks, who did so much to prepare the manuscript; and to Ken Jensen, who took upon himself the lion's share of the work of an editor.

FRED E. BAUMANN

Note

1. Friedrich Nietzsche, *Beyond Good and Evil*, trans. Walter Kaufmann (New York: Vintage Books, 1966), p. 114.

CRIME AND PUNISHMENT

Issues in Criminal Justice

Retribution as the Ground for Punishment

WALTER BERNS

I

It is useful to begin with H. L. A. Hart's "simple" model of a retributive theory of punishment. "Such a theory," Hart writes, "will assert three things: first, that a person may be punished if, and only if, he has voluntarily done something morally wrong; secondly, that his punishment must in some way match, or be the equivalent of, the wickedness of his offence; and thirdly, that the justification for punishing men under such conditions is that the return of suffering for moral evil voluntarily done, is itself just or morally good."[1]

If, then, punishment is the deliberate infliction of pain and legal punishment the infliction of pain on a duly convicted criminal, the right to punish can rest only on the retributive principle so understood. The person punished must deserve the pain inflicted on him. If he has done nothing for which he deserves to suffer, he ought not to be made to suffer; for example, he ought not to be punished solely to deter others from doing something. Of all the statements of this principle, Kant's is probably the most familiar. "Judicial punishment," he wrote, "can never be used merely as a means to promote some other good for the criminal himself or for civil society, but instead it must in all cases be imposed on him only on the ground that he has committed a crime."[2] Magistrates might sometimes be tempted to punish the innocent—for example, when the real malefactors are hard to find—and, so long as their innocence is not known to the public, something useful might be accomplished by doing so, but the retributive principle forbids this. A person's rights protect him from being used merely to influence the behavior of others. After all, human beings are not things, and they are more than animals on which to conduct experiments. Thus, to state this as a principle (and a principle with which most of us can agree), guilt is a necessary condition of punishment.

Kant goes further to argue that guilt is a sufficient condition of punishment. The thief must be incarcerated and be made to work, the slanderer must be publicly humiliated, the murderer must be executed—and all this regardless of utility, which is to say, without regard to whether punishment serves to lower the crime rate or reform the criminal. Kant's is the purest statement of the retributive principle: the criminal must be paid back in kind because he must not be allowed to profit from his wrongdoing. To profit would be unjust to his victim, to civil society, and, indeed, to the criminal himself. How far removed this is from utilitarianism is illustrated in Kant's example of what should be done with murderers: "Even if a civil society were to dissolve itself by common agreement of all its members (for example, if the people inhabiting an island decide to separate and disperse themselves around the world), the last murderer remaining in prison must first be executed, so that everyone will duly receive what his actions are worth and so that the bloodguilt thereof will not be fixed on the people because they failed to insist on carrying out the punishment; for if they fail to do so, they may be regarded as accomplices in this public violation of legal justice."[3]

Understood in this way, retribution strikes some modern writers as not only "disutilitarian" but downright or even perversely foolish. The economist, who is more inclined than other social scientists to weigh things according to their usefulness, objects to retribution because "once a crime has been committed, the costs that it has imposed on society become sunk costs, which cannot be retrieved by punishing the criminal or, for that matter, by doing anything else."[4] The economist is likely to support punishment only if it can be shown to deter others from committing crimes—a theory of punishment that was given its most influential (if not original) statement by Cesare Beccaria, the founder of modern criminology.[5] Writing in the eighteenth century, Beccaria was responsible for the emphasis on civility (thus, on deterrence) in considerations of punishment.

Understood in Kant's way, retribution strikes other modern writers not only as pointless but as pointlessly cruel. From this perspective, talk of criminals deserving punishment or of the moral necessity to pay them back is simply a thinly disguised argument for vengeance. As such, it is said to deserve no place in a modern, compassionate, and enlightened criminal justice system. According to Justice Thurgood Marshall, for example, "punishment as retribution has been condemned by scholars for centuries," ever since the Enlightenment and Beccaria in fact. He also objects to it on constitutional grounds, insisting that the Eighth Amendment (which forbids cruel and unusual punishments) was intended to insulate us "from our baser selves," and that it is the baser self that demands vengeance. As he reads its text, the Constitution forbids "punishment for the sake of retribution."[6]

Marshall is right about Beccaria but wrong about the Constitution. While the Supreme Court from time to time has declared a particular punishment to be cruel and unusual,[7] it has never questioned the propriety of the principle that the punishment must fit the crime; and that principle, embodied in every criminal code or schedule of punishments, is, as Hart pointed out, retributive. It is retributive because it recognizes desert: that criminals deserve to be punished according to the gravity of their crimes. As Kant put it, "only the Law of retribution (*jus talionis*) can determine exactly the kind and degree of punishment."[8] Determining exactly the kind and degree of punishment is more difficult than Kant seems to acknowledge, but some degree of proportionality can be achieved, as Hart points out,[9] and this is sufficient to satisfy at least the more moderate versions of the retributive principle.

II

There is no question but that modern criminologists have held retribution in disrepute. Indeed, they have challenged punishment itself as barbaric and, perhaps worse, unscientific. Thus, not very long ago the leading criminology textbook likened punishing a criminal to punishing "an individual for breathing through his mouth because of enlarged adenoids." This book credited modern scientific penology with having discovered that criminals are not wicked but sick and, if true, that "the guard and jailer [should] be replaced by the nurse, and the judge by the psychiatrist."[10] Similarly, another writer wrote contemptuously of the failure of nineteenth-century penology to forgo its reliance on "violence" and of its continued acceptance of the necessity to exact retribution: "Present-day penology, by contrast, puts its emphasis not on retribution, nor even on deterrence, but on rehabilitation. It combats crime by such reformative and essentially nonpunitive means as probation and psychiatric help in and out of prison. It seeks eventually to replace the old concept of 'the punishment to fit the crime' with a quite new notion: 'the treatment to fit the criminal.' "[11] But quite apart from this faith in science, retribution was discredited because criminologists and jurists were disinclined to admit that anyone deserves, really deserves, anything. For a time at least, criminologists ceased to speak of punishment as just or unjust, reflecting the fashion then reigning among social scientists.

In the vernacular of social science, the old words—*good, evil, just, unjust*—are replaced by the neologisms *value judgment* or, simply, *values*. Like the so-called cultures they are said to be related to or to derive their meaning from, all values are held to be equal. Quite obviously, such usage bespeaks a lack of confidence in the principles of justice embodied in the laws or ways of one's own country—social science will brook no talk of holding certain "truths to be self-evident"—or a lack of commitment to one's own "culture"; and where there is a lack of commitment there is sure to be an absence of will. Without the strength deriving from the confidence that the laws are just, it will be impossible (except with a bad conscience) to punish criminals as they deserve to be punished.

This unwillingness to weigh punishments on the scales of justice was not confined to American writers. Johannes Andenaes, a famous criminologist, quotes a Norwegian judge as saying that "our grandfathers punished, and they did so with a clear conscience [and] we punish too, but we do it with a bad conscience."[12] But, of course, it was primarily the American bad conscience that affected American punishment, and there can be no doubt that there was a bad conscience at work among us. It manifested itself in the accusation that we have no right to punish criminals because it is we who are guilty of the crimes we attribute to them. According to the American Friends Service Committee, for example, most crimes are committed by the "agencies of government," just as most "murders" have been committed by governments.[13] Then, as Tom Wicker of the *New York Times* saw it, Rockefeller was the cause of the Attica prison uprising—not Nelson Rockefeller, the governor of

New York, but the "other Rockefeller—all the Rockefellers of the world, the great owners and proprietors and investors and profitmakers." They had shaped the "society that had produced Attica."[14] Thus, walking in Attica's D-yard in his capacity of "neutral" observer, Wicker ignored the hostages being held by the rioting convicts, listened to the "authentic" eloquence of the convicts' speeches, and threw his arms around the convict who had called out his name, hugging him to his breast. " 'We gonna win, brother,' Wicker says [and these are his own words]. 'We gonna win.' The boy smiled and nodded and Wicker walked on, thinking he was *free at last, free at last*."[15] Then, for one more example of a bad conscience, there was psychiatrist Karl Menninger, who suggested that the only crime we need be concerned with is the "crime of damning some of our fellow citizens with the label 'criminal.' " We do this, he said, because we need crime, or more accurately, we need criminals. We need them to do the "illegal things we *wish* to do and, like scapegoats of old, they bear the burdens of our displaced guilt and punishment."[16] For his work in the field of criminal justice, Menninger won the 1975 Roscoe Pound Prize awarded by the National Institute on Crime and Delinquency.[17]

It should surprise no one to learn that these "advanced" ideas, promulgated by scientists in the textbooks and by intellectuals in the press, found a receptive audience among the judiciary. Judges may cite precedents from the past (giving rise to the myth that they are conservative), but, as Justice William Brennan has admitted, the Supreme Court has become accustomed to being "out in front" of the other branches of government and of public opinion.[18] And trial court judges have learned to behave in like fashion. Judges are by no means the least vain of men and women; on the contrary, they actively seek the approbation of the prestigious press and especially of the major law school faculties, and there is no doubt as to the sort of judicial behavior that earns this approbation. Besides, they have to live with their law clerks, whom these faculties have educated to want to "reform the system" and who in turn educate the judges.

From these various teachers the judges learned that punishment was outmoded; from the American Law Institute in particular they learned that its use should be avoided. Acknowledged to be one of the most influential legal documents of the mid-twentieth century, the Institute's Model Penal Code instructs judges to avoid imprisoning convicted criminals except to incapacitate them, to rehabilitate them, or to avoid depreciating the seriousness of their offenses.[19] What is clear from this is that withholding a sentence of imprisonment was to be the rule and imprisonment the exception. From the Model Sentencing Act, a product of the Council of Judges of the National Council on Crime and Delinquency, the judges received similar advice: except for dangerous offenders, "persons convicted of crime shall be dealt with in accordance with their potential for rehabilitation, considering their individual characteristics, circumstances and needs."[20] That the judges followed the advice of these various experts is suggested by the prison statistics: despite the fact that the number of index crimes known to the police increased from 3,363,700 in 1960 to 8,666,200 in 1973, an increase of 158 percent, there were fewer persons in federal and state prisons in 1973 than in 1960.[21] As I said above, retributive punishment fell into disrepute among criminologists and jurists.

III

Beccaria and that branch of modern criminology which derives from him may denounce retribution as barbaric and intolerable in an enlightened and free society and may argue that society is justified in punishing malefactors only with a view to curing them, incapacitating them, or deterring others from imitating them, but he and his followers have not been able to carry public opinion with them. Typical American citizens will not agree to imposing the equivalent of a traffic fine on a convicted murderer, for example, even knowing that murderers are the least likely to repeat their crimes, or a death sentence on a shoplifter, even if they have reason to believe that this would be a most effective deterrent. Such sentences would be unjust in this popular view, and, unlike some criminologists, citizens persist in speaking of these matters in the language of justice. They demand that criminals be punished not to deter others and emphatically not in order to rehabilitate them (a possibility they tend to deny), but rather to pay them back because criminals deserve to be paid back. C. S. Lewis expressed such views when he wrote: "It is only as deserved or undeserved that a sentence can be just or unjust. I do not here contend that the question 'Is it deserved?' is the only one we can reasonably ask about a punishment. We may very properly ask whether it is likely to deter others and to reform the criminal. But neither of these last two questions is a question about justice. There is no sense in talking about a 'just deterrent' or a 'just cure.'"[22] It is significant that this view, which remained popular, is now beginning to find supporters among criminologists. Indeed, there were intimations of it even in the comment accompanying the publication of the Model Sentencing Act: "some persons, including a few members of the Council of Judges, maintain that punishment *per se* has a proper place in a sentence."[23] This may have portended changes shortly to come: retribution was being rehabilitated.

The reason for this might be traced to the rising crime rate and the growing awareness of the inadequacy of our penal system to cope with it, to a shattering of the hope that modern science (in the forms of psychiatry or social psychology) would find the secret of rehabilitating criminals, or even to a rehabilitation of the sort of conscience that permits punishment of criminals. In any case, one of the country's leading authorities on criminal justice, Norval Morris, now acknowledges that one of the purposes of imprisonment is "properly retributive."[24] Criminals should be made to suffer; that is "a central precept of everyone's sense of justice." And while that may not be literally true—for example, it is doubtful that the modern Quaker or Tom Wicker and Karl Menninger see (or saw) the "link between established crime and deserved suffering"—it is surely true of most citizens. Similar judgments are found in the 1976 Report of the Committee for the Study of Incarceration. Composed of a number of distinguished professors of law, political science, and philosophy, as well as psychiatrists and other scientists, the committee acknowledged that rehabilitation has failed and that, even if it were to succeed, it is unfair insofar as it treats similar cases differently. Besides, "certain things are simply wrong and ought to be punished."[25] It is instructive that the title of this report is *Doing Justice*, and it may be significant that the last few years have seen a dramatic increase in the number of prisoners in state and federal institutions.[26] These studies and these statistics seem to demonstrate a renewed interest in the old-fashioned view (a view never abandoned by most citizens) that criminals deserve to be made to suffer in proportion to the suffering they have inflicted on others. For reasons I shall attempt to elucidate in due course, it is important—even imperative—that the criminal justice system attach great weight to the judgments of most citizens.

IV

The judge who accepts the advice of the Model Sentencing Act—that persons convicted of crimes should be dealt with "in accordance with their potential for rehabilitation, considering their individual characteristics, circumstances and needs"—will quite properly focus on the criminal; aided by the experts in correctional treatment, this judge will try to ascertain what is best for that individual. In the course of building the criminal's psychological profile, examining (sympathetically, of course) the circumstances of his life (past and recent), and hearing testimony as to his needs, the judge is likely to lose sight of the crime and to ignore its victims. Were it not for the old-fashioned ways of the office, the judge might even descend from the bench and, like Tom Wicker, embrace the so-called criminal and call him "brother." A generous description of this process might be: doing mercy.

Doing justice, however, requires the judge to focus on the crime and the suffering it caused. The difference between doing justice and doing mercy or doing something useful is well stated in the Report of the Committee for the Study of Incarceration: "to assert that someone deserves to be punished is to look to his past wrongdoing as reason for having him penalized. This orientation to the past distinguishes desert from the other purported aims of punishment—deterrence, incapacitation, rehabilitation—which seek to justify the criminal sanction by its prospective usefulness in preventing crime."[27] The criminal justice reformers focused on the criminal and the future; most citizens focus on the crime committed in the past and on the suffering it caused. They are remembering those events when, typically, they demand that criminals be paid back. The ground of this demand is the simple yet wholly respectable opinion that justice consists in giving people, the good as well as the bad, what they deserve. And if these citizens are at all reflective, they will understand that it is not only right for the criminal to suffer but wrong to deprive law-abiding persons of the satisfaction of knowing that the criminal has been made to suffer. Here is Adam Smith on this subject: "Our sense of the horror and dreadful atrocity of [the conduct of a Borgia or Nero], the delight which we take in hearing that it was properly punished, the indignation which we feel when it escapes this due retaliation, our whole sense and feeling, in short, of its ill desert, of the propriety and fitness of inflicting evil upon the person who is guilty of it, and of making him grieve in turn, arises from the sympathetic indignation which naturally boils up in the breast of the spectator, whenever he thoroughly brings home to himself the case of the sufferer."[28]

Rather than acknowledge that what he is describing is the desire to exact revenge ("the most detestable of the passions"), Smith, perhaps in order to tame the passion by giving it another name, calls it resentment. But is it really resentment that, to choose his example, prompts us "to desire, not only that [the murderer of our father or brother] should be punished, but that he should be punished by our means," or to feel "cheated" if he should die a natural death before being punished by us, which is to say, by the law? Would it not be more accurate to describe the passion at work here as anger? If so, it is not sufficient to agree with Justice Thurgood Marshall that the desire to retaliate against criminals comes "from our baser selves"; anger is the uniquely human passion that leads us to cry out for justice.

Anger is expressed only by human beings against other human beings. It is expressed when someone has acted unjustly or is thought to have acted unjustly. One of its bases is the idea that human beings, unlike other beings, should be held responsible for what they do. As Aristotle may have been the first to notice,[29] anger is accompanied not only by the pain caused by and attributed to others but also by the pleasure arising from the hope of retaliating against them, or paying them back as they deserve to be paid back. As I have written elsewhere, "We can become angry with an inanimate object (the door we run into and then kick in return) only by foolishly attributing responsibility to it, and we cannot do that for long, which is why we do not think of returning later to revenge ourselves on the door."[30] For the same reason, we cannot be more than momentarily angry with a dog, and we tend to pity rather than be angry with human beings who are not responsible for their acts (for example, because they are insane). Rather than coming "from our baser selves," anger expresses an element of the soul that harbors the view that there is responsibility in the world. In holding particular people responsible or accountable, anger pays them the respect due them as human beings. It recognizes that only human beings are moral beings, and in this way anger demonstrates its connection with justice.

It is easy to condemn anger and necessary to condemn it when it becomes excessive or uncontrolled. We know of angry children, angry legislators, and angry mobs, and it is essential that they be controlled—the first by parents, the second by rules of order, and the third by the law. But even if it is true, as I think it is, that the demand for revenge comes out of anger, it does not follow that an effort should be made to excise anger from the human soul as Hobbes tried to do with pride.

For anger, like pride, has its attractive as well as its unattractive elements. Better, then, to follow Madison's advice for dealing with "the mischiefs of faction": attempt not to remove its causes (which lie in the passions) but, rather, to control its effects.[31] Like the self-love which was Madison's principal concern, anger can prove useful when properly controlled and directed. Indeed, retribution, which comes out of anger, can be both just and useful. Just as self-love, in Madison's analysis, can serve to promote national prosperity and with it free government, so retribution can serve to promote law-abidingness and thereby to preserve free government.

It is sometimes said—by Freud, for example—that anger is simply a selfish passion, rather like greed, and of course it can be that. The athlete who is fouled or is wrongly penalized for committing a foul will be angry for selfish reasons; so, too, will be those who have suffered at the hands of criminals. Such examples could readily be multiplied. But is it a selfish public that is angry with and demands revenge against Charles Manson and his "family," killers of actress Sharon Tate, or Richard Speck, cold-blooded killer of eight Chicago student nurses; or Lee Harvey Oswald, the likely killer of President Kennedy; or James Earl Ray, killer of Martin Luther King? There were many angry Americans, white as well as black, when King was murdered, and the vast majority of them were not personally connected with King. In itself this may not be sufficient to refute the charge that anger is merely a selfish passion, but if this manifest expression of concern for the fate of others is said ultimately to be a sign of concern for oneself, then the same will have to be said of compassion and pity, which are manifest expressions of concern for the condition of others. Indeed, the same would have to be said—and Hobbes said it[32]—of all expressions or manifestations of concern for others: namely, that they arise out of a concern for oneself alone. Nevertheless, speaking politically, if we are not saddened when a fellow being (and especially a fellow citizen) suffers, or angry when he or she suffers unjustly, then we might properly be charged with selfishness; that would require us to recognize that the polity (our particular part of the human community) is in trouble. The polity needs charity, which depends on compassion or pity; it also needs justice, which depends on anger—whether on the part of heroes in the presence of foreign enemies or common citizens in the presence of domestic criminals.

Does compassion, like anger, inherently combine with the pain aroused by the suffering of others an element of pleasure—for example, the pleasure of knowing that there but for the grace of God go I? There can be little doubt that a reputation for compassion gives pleasure to the person who bears it. This is proved almost daily by our politicians, almost all of whom claim to be compassionate and urge the rest of us to join them. Compassion is now regarded as a virtue and seems to be more highly praised than courage, moderation, justice, or prudence. It certainly has a better press than anger, despite the fact that it shares with anger the capability to be misdirected. For the truth is that it is possible both to be angry with and feel compassion for persons who have done nothing or little to deserve one or the other. As Clifford Orwin said, in a superb analysis of compassion, "neither good nor bad in itself, [compassion like anger] will be better or worse depending on the moral education and character of the person who feels it."[33]

Without an investigation requiring more effort than the subject deserves, it is not possible to decide whether Tom Wicker was moved more by guilt or by compassion as he moved among the prisoners in the Attica D-yard. It was surely guilt that led him to blame Rockefeller and the other "great owners and proprietors and investors and profit-makers" for the prison riot—after all, he would have to include himself or at least his associates at the *New York Times* among these capitalist malefactors—but it was just as surely compassion that led him to embrace that prisoner and call him "brother." Guilt and compassion, but not a sense of justice. After all, Wicker had no knowledge whatever of the crimes committed by that prisoner; as an editor of the country's most influential and comprehensive newspaper, however, he ought to have known that the typical inmate in a New York maximum security prison has committed some heinous crime indeed. For the guards being held hostage he felt no compassion whatever; he reserved that for the prisoners, and in so doing he acted as the compassionate tend to act in our day. For if it is typical citizens who respond angrily in the presence of crime, it is typically intellectuals who respond with compassion not for the criminal's victims but for the criminal. The former live among the victims—walk their streets, ride their subways, and play in their parks—and can readily imagine sharing the victims' fate. For this reason, their anger might indeed be attributed to a concern for themselves. The latter, their souls cluttered with an assortment of ideological debris as isolated from the victims as from the crimes that torment them, find it pleasant as well as safe to feel compassion for the convicted criminal who is, after all, suffering or is about to suffer. It makes them feel good—for this reason, such compassion might be attributed to their concern for themselves—and it exacts no price in return. "The boy smiled and nodded and Wicker walked on, thinking he was *free at last, free at last*"—and then, pleased with himself for this display of humanity, returned to his safe haven. Unlike morality or doing good, which always involves some self-denial or self-restraint, compassion is easy. As Orwin says, it charms more and chafes less than morality. It emphasizes gratifying others rather than denying oneself. A true Christian, says Rousseau, is hard on himself and easy on others. A mellow person can be easy on both. Compassion is expansive, not puritanical; except where maddened by guilt, it does not cramp our style. The issue for the criminal justice system is whether to respond to the citizen's anger or the intellectual's compassion. In fact, it is no contest.

If it is to preserve the moral community, the law must punish the criminal, thereby satisfying the anger expressed by its law-abiding citizens. More is involved here than what I shall call preemption, by which I mean the necessity to act in order to prevent private citizens from taking the law into their own hands. As I said, that anger is made up of the pain caused by the criminal (and it is right to feel that pain) and of the pleasure arising from the hope that the criminal will be made to suffer pain in return (and it is right to feel that pleasure). Call it vengeance or even, in the words of the late Herbert L. Packer, "blood lust," but it is right to feel it. As Packer says, when properly tamed, anger reinforces individual rectitude. "When the criminal is seen caught up in the toils of the [legal] process, any desire people may have that he suffer reinforces the values against which he has offended."[34] Thus, contrary to Beccaria and the generations of criminologists he influenced, retribution is not useless; like deterrence, but operating in a different way, it is useful. The one deters crime by promising to impose pain; the other promotes law-abidingness by making it pleasurable. Law-abidingness is a very useful habit in a society that wants to remain free, and it is appropriate that the law promote it.

As the ancients knew very well, the criminal law does its work by praising as well as by blaming. It blames crime when it punishes the criminal and, by thereby giving pleasure to the angry, it praises law-abidingness. Retributive punishment is the response to the anger that is properly aroused by crime.

Notes

1. H. L. A. Hart, *Punishment and Responsibility: Essays in the Philosophy of Law* (New York and Oxford: Oxford University Press, 1968), p. 231.
2. Immanuel Kant, *The Metaphysical Elements of Justice*, trans. John Ladd (Indianapolis: Bobbs-Merrill, Library of Liberal Arts, 1965), p. 100.
3. Ibid., p. 102.
4. Richard A. Posner, "Retribution and Related Concepts of Punishment," *Journal of Legal Studies* 9 (January 1980): 74.
5. Cesare Beccaria, *On Crimes and Punishment*, trans. Henry Paolucci (Indianapolis: Bobbs-Merrill, Library of Liberal Arts, 1963; originally published in 1764).
6. *Furman* v. *Georgia*, 408 U.S. 238, 343–44 (1972).
7. For example, *Weems* v. *United States*, 217 U.S. 349 (1910); *Trop* v. *Dulles*, 346 U.S. 86 (1958).
8. Kant, *Metaphysical Elements*, p. 101.
9. Hart, *Punishment and Responsibility*, pp. 231–33.
10. Edwin H. Sutherland and Donald R. Cressey, *Principles of Criminology*, 7th ed. (Philadelphia and New York: Lippincott, 1966), p. 366.
11. Giles Playfair, "Is the Death Penalty Necessary?" in *Capital Punishment*, ed. Grant A. McClellan (New York: H.W. Wilson, 1961), p. 128.
12. Johannes Andenaes, *Punishment and Deterrence*, (Ann Arbor: University of Michigan Press, 1974), p. 133.
13. American Friends Service Committee, *Struggle for Justice* (New York: Hill & Wang, 1971), p. 10.
14. Tom Wicker, *A Time to Die* (New York: Quadrangle, 1975), p. 203.
15. Ibid., pp. 248–49. Italics in the original.
16. Karl Menninger, *The Crime of Punishment* (New York: Viking, 1969), p. 153. Italics in original.
17. *American Journal of Corrections* 37 (July–August 1975): 32.
18. Bob Woodward and Scott Armstrong, *The Brethren: Inside the Supreme Court* (New York: Simon & Schuster, 1979), p. 254.
19. *Model Penal Code*, proposed final draft (Philadelphia: American Law Institute, 1962), p. 106.
20. National Council on Crime and Delinquency, Council of Judges, Model Sentencing Act, art. 1, in *Crime and Delinquency* 18 (1972): 335–370, esp. p. 344.
21. *Sourcebook of Criminal Justice Statistics* (Washington, D.C.: U.S. Department of

Justice, 1974), pp. 434, 471. There were 212,953 prisoners in 1960 and 204,349 in 1973.

22. C. S. Lewis, "The Humanitarian Theory of Punishment," in *God in the Dock: Essays on Theology and Ethics*, ed. Walter Hooper (Grand Rapids: Eerdmans, 1973), p. 288.

23. Model Sentencing Act, in *Crime and Delinquency* 18 (1972): 344.

24. Norval Morris, "The Future of Imprisonment: Toward a Punitive Philosophy," *Michigan Law Review* 72 (May 1974): 1161.

25. Andrew von Hirsch, *Doing Justice: The Choice of Punishments* (New York: Hill & Wang, 1976), pp. xxxix, 18, and passim.

26. At the end of 1979, there were 314,006 prisoners in state and federal facilities (not counting another 6,497 who were being held in local jails because of overcrowding)—an increase of 109,657 or 54 percent in six years. *Sourcebook of Criminal Justice Statistics* (Washington, D.C.: U.S. Department of Justice, 1981), pp. 477, 469.

27. Von Hirsch, *Doing Justice*, p. 46.

28. Adam Smith, *The Theory of Moral Sentiments* (New York: Augustus Kelly, 1966), pp. 107–8.

29. Aristotle, *Rhetoric* 1378b1–5.

30. Walter Berns, *For Capital Punishment: Crime and the Morality of the Death Penalty* (New York: Basic Books, 1979), p. 153. I have borrowed much in this section from this source.

31. *Federalist* 10.

32. Hobbes, *Leviathan*, chap. 6.

33. Clifford Orwin, "Compassion," *American Scholar* 49 (Summer 1980): 309–33.

34. Herbert L. Packer, *The Limits of the Criminal Sanction* (Stanford, Calif.: Stanford University Press, 1968), pp. 33–44. See also Emile Durkheim, *The Division of Labor in Society*, trans. George Simpson (Glencoe, Ill.: Free Press, 1933), pp. 87–109; and Gabriel Tarde, *Penal Philosophy*, trans. Rapelje Howell (Montclair, N.J.: Patterson Smith, 1968), pp. 35, 37, 77, 505, and passim.

Moral Science, Social Science, and the Idea of Justice

DANIEL N. ROBINSON

The argument of this essay may be summarized briefly as advancing the following propositions: (*a*) the idea of justice strictly entails terms of an irreducibly moral nature; (*b*) the alleged relativity of such terms, though metaphysically arguable, is incompatible with a regime of justice; and (*c*) the methods, perspectives, and, in most instances, findings of the social sciences are irrelevant to the aims of justice and at variance with its character. The defense of these propositions brings under suspicion a number of current "received truths," among which are claims to the effect that law is an essentially social institution and justice an essentially utilitarian enterprise. Other current maxims found to be defective or incoherent are those pertaining to putatively "natural" rights.

I

Attempts to date the birth of an idea arise from a scholarly passion that is doomed to remain unrequited. When the search is confined, however, to what may be called the institutional history of an idea, at least a partial success often is within reach. In the instance of justice, a good case can be made for the ancient Greek world of Draco and his successor, Solon. They are, of course, the most famous of the ancient Archons, Draco having had a much worse press than his record actually warrants. But in deference to fashion and for the sake of brevity, we can distinguish between the Homeric and the Solonic epochs of justice.

The etymology of *justice*—*dike*—is revealing. In its earliest acceptation, *dike* refers only to a divided path, a choice-point along a journey. In the Homeric epics as well as in Hesiod's *Works and Days* it is common for *right* and *wrong* to express no more than the path chosen for the actor by the gods. Thus was the idea of justice entirely absorbed into the religious beliefs and convictions of the age. The grave offense of hubris was just that which displeased the gods or, worse, excited their envy. What made such actions wrong was nothing beyond the divine retribution they elicited.

During the long tribal or phratric seasons of pre-Hellenic Greek culture, nothing more rational than custom was invoked as the means for settling disputes and, as it were, conducting business. Criminal actions committed by any member of one phratry against any member of another were avenged according to the "principle," which is to say the *dogma*, of group liability. With Draco, however, and even more officially with Solon, all of this was swept aside and replaced by the doctrine of personal responsibility. This was a momentous shift in human history, and it allows us to date (with the usual reservations) the dawn of an individualistic psychology grounded in the recognition that persons are at least to some degree autonomous. Centuries later, reflecting on this autonomy—this *auto nomos* or capacity for self-rule—the Athenian Stranger in Plato's *Laws* (1.644) acknowledges that a person is manipulated like a puppet by the gods, but there is one cord he can pull "against all the rest; and this is the sacred and golden cord of reason."

In moving away from phratric or tribal notions of justification, ancient Greece lifted itself above the level of mere culture and to the heights of a bona fide civilization. It took on, that is, powers of influence that would survive its own military, commercial, and political destruction. The recognition of individual autonomy aroused individual initiative and liberated the beneficiary from the constricted perimeter of group thought. It is not merely fortuitous that this now-liberated age would yield the first historians. Only when human beings took for granted that they made history, that they made a difference in what happened in the world, did it make sense to record the past.

The issue marked out by the terms *freedom* and *determinism* has been central in the history of speculation and has not even been confined to the realm of human actions. The pre-Socratic physicists and their descendants all the way down to our own time can be seen weighing the competing claims of a purely statistical and an utterly determined material universe. Note, then, that freedom from determination does not entail a moral quality, for it may refer to no more than the intrinsic, statistical, and uncertain dynamics of matter in motion—the dynamics which are described, at a causal level, as accidents. The moral dimension is engaged only when there is the presumption that certain actions (events) are free not only in the sense of not being governed by the laws that regulate matter but also in the sense of being nonaccidental.

The history of mixing or conflating physical and psychological principles is ancient. The Socratics' well-known distrust of the senses arose partly from the arguments Heracleitus had developed to show the endless flux suffered by the world of matter. The ancient philosophers, like their modern descendants, can be found on all sides of the freedom-determinism issue. Those who answer to the name *radical determinists* can find no exception to the operation of causal factors in the origin of any and every event, including events we identify with a specific person. Others, then and now, may be called *soft determinists* in that they leave no room for freedom in the purely physical realm but a modest degree of autonomy in the realms of human action. And still others, in the patrimony of Heracleitus, see only chance, change, and probability in the affairs of men and of atoms. "Nemo descensit bis in idem fluminem."

These several possibilities are tenable, if not equally so, at the purely metaphysical level, but only one view is coherent and plausible at the level of a civilized social life: if there is to be law at all, the presumption of human autonomy is inescapable. To write a law that proscribes actions of a certain sort is, among other considerations, to acknowledge that such actions are possible. It is to acknowledge further that they are not the inevitable consequence of the sort of causal series we take to be behind events of a merely physical nature. The very act of legislation—of declaring "Thou shalt not"—can be plausibly directed only at those who have within their power the ability to act and to withhold actions in ways that violate or respect the requirements of law.

It might be contended at this juncture that the binding force of law is the threat of punishment and, therefore, that compliance is totally determined by the pleasure-seeking, pain-avoiding instincts or inclinations of all creatures, including humans. This is defective as a rebuttal in several ways. First, to establish that an action arose from threats or promises shows not that the action was externally determined but that the actor chose reward over punishment. After all, if the freedom to choose is denied across the board, there could be no basis on which to explain or understand the reliability with which rewards and punishments do influence behavior. Moreover, determinists would have no point in exhorting us to accept this thesis unless they were willing to acknowledge that we are able to choose their metaphysics over competing ones.

As a statement of fact the hedonistic theory also fails, for there are numerous instances of heedless actions, heroic actions, and conduct that simply ignores the cost/benefit calculus. To judge such actions as irrational or imprudent or pointless is, however, to invoke standards of rationality, prudence, and intentionality, standards that are intelligible only within the context of autonomy.

As an inference from the deterministic laws of physics, the hedonistic theory of compliance also fails to weaken the concept of human autonomy, for it is just this concept that is offered to challenge the theory of determinism or, more generally, the theory according to which humanity is but another form of physical system. A theory according to which "X is not a member of the set Y" is not refuted by the mere insistence that "everything is a member of Y." There is, after all, an important difference between answering and begging a question. Additionally, since there is no evidence of needs or motives on the part of those physical entities said to be determined by the laws of physics, it isn't at all clear how even the hedonistic motives are like physical forces.

The determinist who chooses realism over metaphor will accept that there are differences between physical events and human actions and will grant that the latter do, indeed, proceed from motives, reasons, and other ingredients of choice. What is denied, then, is not human rationality or human purposes but the claim that these are undetermined. Instead, these too are brought about by the preceding and concurrent physical events taking place in the brain. Thus, although at the psychological level we may continue to speak of reasons, motives, purposes, and the like, the scientific explanation of them must inevitably come from the discovery of underlying (neural) causes.

The nature of the relationship between neurological and mental events remains the *quaestio vexata* of philosophy of mind, and this is surely not the place to settle the matter. It is sufficient to recognize that the entire issue is very much alive and that all the confident "solutions" of the mind/body problem are hopelessly defective. What is important to keep in mind is that both radical environmental determinism and radical biological determinism are, if true, inconsequential. The more radical the determinism is, the more inconsequential it must be. If, alas, every human action is determined—every thought, every emotion, every belief—then this theory also is determined, as is its reception. It is in the most literal respect an inconsequential theory because neither accepting nor denying it can have consequences. It is a form of what John Stuart Mill called "Asiatic fatalism," and its legislative authority makes all metaphysical quibbles nugatory. Far from rendering our laws and punishments pointless, it makes them inevitable.

Radical determinism thus is inconsequential if true and to be ignored if false. Moreover, when its metaphysical claws are removed, leaving it in the state of a soft and pliable determinism, it does not raise a challenge against the principles of justice but instead actually helps to explain their foundation. Soft determinism asserts that significant human actions are to some degree guided, even impelled, by factors not of the actor's own choosing and of which the actor may occasionally be ignorant. Put another way, soft determinism avers that actions do not invariably reflect pure rationality and the rational choices it makes possible. Instead, the actor may be in the clutches of anger, greed, lust, indolence, indifference, and those other states that conflict with the choice of just ends and just means to them. This is all true and was, we may be sure, fully appreciated by all the tribes of mankind long before the dawn of metaphysics. If every human being were a veritable saint of reason—if actions never proceeded but on a disinterested and rational basis—the law would be unnecessary. And if, on the other hand, no one ever has had the ability, the freedom, to regulate his or her own conduct, the law would be no more than an empty ritual.

The idea of justice emerges from the recognition that some actions fall within the perimeter of the actor's free choices in that there is no known law of nature making them inevitable. Because they are able to choose a course of conduct, and only because of this, actors can be described as either praiseworthy or blameworthy. And it is in precisely this sense that the idea of justice entails terms of an irreducibly moral nature, for the terms *praise* and *blame* are unintelligible outside the moral context. What is specifically rejected here is what is sometimes called the emotive theory of morals, the theory according to which moral attributions reflect no more than the emotional or temperamental states induced by actions of a certain kind. To praise or blame an actor it is minimally necessary: (*a*) to regard the action as intended, (*b*) to weigh the aptness or worthiness of the intended goal, and (*c*) to assess the overall and prevailing conditions surrounding the actions themselves. Neither regarding, weighing, nor assessing falls within the province of the emotions; these are deliberative functions which require rationality. To judge an action as blameworthy may also involve righteous indignation or some other sentiment, but the judgment must be grounded in an awareness that a principle has been violated. The emotive theory of moral attributions fails to make the necessary distinction between rationality and its (occasional) affective consequences.

To say that an actor has chosen a course of action is also to acknowledge that the action has some goal or objective. What the actor must assemble is a means-end strategy such that the events following an action can be plausibly regarded as expressions of the actor's intentions. Nature yields two general classes of conduct of a means-end sort: the class generally regarded as instinctive and the class recognized as available only to rational creatures. We make distinctions between these two classes on several grounds. Behavior is regarded as instinctive when (*a*) it is displayed universally within a given species by either sex or by both sexes; (*b*) it appears in the absence of specific training and only after a period of maturation; (*c*) it is very highly heritable in the sense that it can be affected by radical alterations of the organism's genetic composition; and (*d*) it is highly stereotypical or ritualistic and thus can be broken down into a series of specific steps, each of which is typically essential to the appearance of the next. Instinctive behavior is governed by those biochemical and neurophysiological processes grounded in the genetic nuances of species. As such, this behavior is an expression of just those laws of nature over which human justice can exercise no moderating influence. From the legal-moral point of view, instinctive behavior is indistinguishable from tidal waves, rainfall, and the motion of the planets.

The conduct taken as arising from rationality is different from this in all ways except one. It is not universally displayed by members of the species; it does not appear suddenly, after a specific period of maturation and in the absence of any and all training; it is not highly stereotypical but wonderfully protean and diverse. It is, however, heritable, in the sense both of being species specific and of being vulnerable to drastic genetic alterations, as in the case of genetically induced mental retardation. Where this retardation is profound, the actions forthcoming are more akin to instincts and are so lacking in rational foundations as to render the actor legally and morally immune. The *non compos mentis* (no power of mind) of ancient Roman law was invoked chiefly in cases such as this.

The division of conduct into the categories of instinctive and rational proceeds from Kant's famous dichotomy of the natural and the intelligible realms. Man as a material entity falls fully within the province of nature and is governed ineluctably by nature's laws. But man as a moral and rational entity, endowed with the sense of right and wrong and with an intellect capable of framing categorical propositions, also occupies that intelligible realm in which the material-causal laws of nature play no part.

It is precisely because we occupy both realms that our "moral science" must be incomplete and perhaps forever arguable. As creatures of nature, we are impelled by natural forces as these affect the chemistry and physiology of our purely biological lives. We are the victims of rage, intemperance, sloth, greed, distraction, envy. Whether such inclinations and passions rise to the public level of conduct depends in the last analysis on the degree to which our rationality is dispository. It is, alas, one of the primary functions of law to enlarge the domain of human conduct answerable to the dictates of reason. And the law performs this function chiefly by regarding us as rational beings and by holding us responsible for our actions—even though we may be angry, intemperate, slothful, and so on. What the law says, in so many words, is that although we are animals, we are not merely animals. Our significant social actions are not in the thrall of instinct, and civilization is more than the discipline of the ant heap.

II

The alleged relativity of justice and morals has been defended on a variety of grounds, some overlapping and all arising from a combination of defective metaphysics, simplistic psychology, and the abuse of science. For present purposes it is sufficient to assess the major themes of current moral relativism without pausing for a lengthy and unavoidably technical review of its history.

So-called natural law theory and its supporting "normative" ethics have attracted criticism from the time of their origins in Greek antiquity and their flourishing in thirteenth-century (medieval) Europe. The version of the long debate for which our own century will be remembered centers on positivistic theories of jurisprudence and utilitarian theories of ethics. Both trends have deep roots in eighteenth- and nineteenth-century thought. The chief arguments for utilitarianism were well developed in David Hume's major works and were given more precise contours in the writings of Jeremy Bentham and John Stuart Mill. I have discussed these developments at length elsewhere.[1] Positivism has had a more winding history—from the somewhat innocent scientism of Saint-Simon and his disciple, Auguste Comte, through the empiriocriticism of Ernst Mach, to that formidable Tower of Babel occupied by the luminaries of the Vienna Circle. It is of some interest that the leading jurists and lawyers of America began to commit themselves to "legal positivism" at just about the time philosophers were convinced that the philosophical wellspring was, alas, dry as a bone.

The initial aim of the logical positivists (Moritz Schlick, Otto Neurath, Phillip Frank, et al.) was to retain that quite radically empiricistic character which Mach had demanded of science, while at the same time basing the language and the explanations of science on a totally logicomathematical foundation. What the school set out to do, in a word, was to strip science of all that was metaphysical by translating both its methods and its achievements into the metaphysically neutral and antiseptic argot of logic. The proposition or slogan that reflected this commitment—taking the lead from Ludwig Wittgenstein—was, *The meaning of a proposition is identical to the method of its verification.* Through verificationism, propositions would be kept utterly empirical or exposed as literally nonsensical. Thus, a claim that an action is ethically wrong either is nonsensical—in that it appeals to no possible experiential confirmation—or refers to some reliable experiential correlate of the action, such as feelings of disapproval or loathing. Note that the well-known emotive theory of ethics is a trivial deduction from the larger premises of positivism.

It wasn't too long before members of the Circle recognized that verificationism itself must also be nonsensical ("unscientific"), for there is no empirical means by which to verify the proposition according to which its meaning is identical to its method of verification! Still worse, verificationism accepts as quite sensible ("scientific") such disjunctions as, *Either dogs have nine legs or the moon is made of cheese.* But clearly worst of all, verificationism required that every scientific law be characterized as meaningless and nonsensical, for every such law is a universal proposition (for example, $F = m \times a$) which can never be exhaustively verified in experience.

Although legal positivism, in the patrimony of Kelson, Holmes, and others, still enjoys wide support in jural settings—including the support of those who have probably never read a page of philosophy of law—the parent *ism* suffered quiet burial at least thirty years ago. Just the slogan now survives, and this only in realms of discourse in which philosophical rigor is replaced by social engineering. When we learn, for example, that "you can't legislate morality," or that legislation must honor the "pluralistic" composition of America, we are witnessing the deformed progeny of positivism: an ethics that can find no support beyond the shifting and ambiguous feelings of the mob; an epistemology tied to nothing more durable or certain than the latest polls. What the defenders of these utterances must fall back on, and do fall back on when pressed, is the contention that all propositions find their truth in the experience of the beholder. Indeed, if the defenders are dated in their reading habits, they may go so far as to proclaim that "the meaning of a proposition is identical to its method of verification." Since the only trusted mode of verification is experience—and experience is a notoriously subjective affair—all ethical propositions are relative to the experiences, personal feelings, and unduplicated biographies of the governed. (Note, by the way, that in this universalized form, ethical relativism is self-refuting—again, experience can never exhaustively verify the claims of a universal proposition.)

It was never necessary, of course, to show that logical positivism was a defective philosophy of science in order to recognize its inapplicability to law and morals. Only the most daring metaphysical leaps can bridge the vast space that separates jural-moral discourse and reasoning from the discourse and reasoning of the natural sciences. To date, all who have attempted this leap have never made it to the other side, and this for the soundest Kantian reasons (*vide supra*). The American Constitution, for example, is a congeries of nonsense on strict positivistic grounds, and the Declaration of Independence—bloated as it is with "self-evident truths"!—is preposterous on these same grounds.

Utilitarianism is another of the "experience philosophies" seeking to place morals and jurisprudence on a foundation untainted by metaphysical and transcendent considerations. Although it has come a long way since Bentham's formulation of the pleasure principle, it retains its attachment to the original proposition according to which *good* and *evil* have no meaning beyond the actual consequences that actions have on real persons. Thus, to classify an action as right or wrong, good or evil, it is necessary to calculate the net happiness (or suffering) occasioned by that action. According to act-utilitarianism, this calculation is called for in the case of each particular act: *It is unjust for me to lie to Jones because of the suffering it will cause him.* According to rule-utilitarianism, the calculation must take into account the overall consequences of actions of a certain kind: *It is unjust to lie, for over the long run, lying yields net suffering.* For both the act- and the rule-utilitarian, however, all injunctions against deceit would be dispelled on the first showing that good consequences would follow. There is in this philosophy, then, no commitment to truths or facts per se, which would seem to be as telling an indictment against a school of philosophy as criticism can summon.

It is all too habitual in utilitarian treatises for defenders to conflate historical and moral dimensions. Hume and Bentham were inclined to take the (alleged) historical fact of the sovereignty of the pleasure principle in human affairs as its sufficient justification. With Mill there is a transition from treating utility as what always has been the case to what ought to be the case. It is scarcely surprising that Mill, thoroughly committed to political reform, would not seek to justify a system of ethics on merely traditional grounds. But what Mill never adequately answered is the question of why we ought to promote human happiness. His answer was drawn from naturalism, but it scarcely follows from the (alleged) fact that human beings always pursue their happiness that (*a*) others ought to assist them or (*b*) the pursuit itself is just. Morals proceed from a set of propositions, not from a set of facts.

Mill arrived at utilitarianism primarily through his own flawed associationistic psychology—an early behaviorism—whose liabilities were less obvious in 1850 than they are now. Convinced that the mind is no more than a repository of current and recalled experiences and their various combinations, Mill insisted that social philosophy take its direction from empirical psychology. (With a strained consistency, he went so far as to argue that even abstract mathematics is a purely inductive matter, leading Jean Piaget a century later to observe that, according to the radical empiricist, the series of positive integers was discovered one at a time!)

Any number of objections to utilitarianism have been framed in terms of the counterintuitive results it produces. Suppose, for example, that a destructive mob can be appeased only by the execution of a prisoner known by the authorities to be innocent. This single execution can be shown to prevent a riot that will take many lives. (John Rawls has coined the term *telishment* to cover punishments justified on the basis of a larger goal, *telos*.) Today's utilitarians seem to find nothing wrong with the execution apart from the long-range negative consequences resulting from the public's knowledge that an innocent person has been hanged. The bickering seems to center on whether the authorities could ever guarantee total secrecy!

But it is rather beside the point that utilitarianism allows counterintuitive justifications. More to the point, does it seek to explain rights, duties, justifications, and so on, or doesn't it? If not, then utilitarianism is simply beyond the perimeter of legal-moral concerns. If, however, it does, then it finds itself referring to entities having no empirical reference at all. One cannot experience a right or duty or obligation. There is, as a matter of strict empirical fact, no such thing as a natural right. Any claim we might make to having a knowledge of such entities cannot arise from our sensations, be they visual or visceral. Rights and duties are irreducible moral terms that cannot be translated into affections of the nerves or the body. They are the product of propositional and not empirical sequences. In a word, they proceed from arguments of an essentially syllogistic form.[2]

This frequently neglected aspect of jural and moral reasoning can be illustrated through one of the enduring maxims of law and morals: *The innocent shall go unpunished*. Why is this so? And here I make not the factual claim that innocent persons have never been punished but the moral claim that it is never justified to punish those known to be innocent. To understand what would be defective in a law that is indifferent to the guilt or innocence of those punished under it, it is only necessary to appreciate the nature of law itself. Law, as discussed earlier, proceeds from the assumption of human autonomy—the assumption that the actions proscribed by law are actions over which persons have control. The knowing punishment of the innocent, therefore, is logically incompatible with the concept of law, quite apart from any long-term or short-term consequences such punishment might produce. The law, in holding persons responsible, implies and logically entails the categories of guilt and innocence and thus cannot be at once coherent as a concept and at the same time indifferent to these very categories.

The connection between law and morals is direct and unambiguous in a just state, justice here regarded as the law taking counsel from moral reasoning. There can, therefore, be unjust laws precisely because a given statute—a given regime—might depart significantly from fundamental moral canons. The canons themselves emerge from the most basic considerations of human rationality and autonomy. As Kant noted, the only perfectly moral being must be a perfectly rational being. All of the actions of such a being would be directed by what Aristotle called the royal rule of reason, a reason in possession of principles and having the power to comprehend all the implications flowing from those principles.

Reason in this sublunary space is less than perfect and so too, therefore, are our moral reckonings. Accordingly, there is always room for the enlargement of justice through legislation and adjudication. But note that this enlargement is not the gift of feelings or passions or popular enthusiasms. Rather, it springs chiefly from the rational appraisal of the connections (or lack thereof) between a given policy or practice and a given universal moral postulate. Thus, that *the innocent shall go unpunished* is accepted as a universal moral postulate is reason enough to outlaw the victimization of entire racial groups. To punish a person for being black or brown or red is to punish him for an attribute over which he could exercise no control and to treat him not as a morally autonomous being but as something indistinguishable from the larger group to which he has been arbitrarily assigned. Slavery did not become wrong only when Congress ratified the Thirteenth Amendment. It was *always* wrong as long as the maxim *the innocent shall go unpunished* was recognized as a fundamental principle of justice. Slavery was wrong before the amendment was proposed or ratified; it was wrong during the long seasons when slavery found favor among the ruling majorities; it would be wrong if the slaves themselves desired it. The rightness or wrongness of an action or policy is determined by the principle it honors or contradicts. The question must always be, *What is the principle?* and not *How many are in favor?*

In regarding natural rights as "nonsense on stilts," Jeremy Bentham was recording his opposition to transcendental elements in jurisprudence. He found, in the history of the human longings for happiness, a more realistic approach to understanding the basis upon which laws appear and are obeyed or overturned. His attention to the purely useful and hedonic dimensions of law was simplistic, but his recognition of the nonempirical nature of natural rights was acute and faultless. Such alleged rights are literally nonsense in that no datum of sense experience is attached to them. They are raised to the heights of truth only on the stilts of the metaphysician.

It is one of the irksome paradoxes of today's liberal rhetoric that the now-swollen category of natural rights is defended by those who celebrate our pluralistic society and who proclaim the relativity of morals. The paradox, of course, is that it is only by way of moral *absolutes* that any of the rights in question can come into being in the first instance. One may take any of the raging issues of the day—ERA, affirmative action, desegregation of schools, school busing, the rights of homosexuals, church-state separation, freedom of the press—and, on the relativistic and pluralistic construing of morals, simply declare that (*a*) women shall not have the same privileges as men enjoy, (*b*) black and white children will be educated separately, (*c*) homosexuals will be punished, (*d*) the government will represent the wishes of the Christian majority, and (*e*) the press will publish what the nation wishes to read. The point, of course, is that *a relativistic morality will sustain only a majoritarian politics*, in fact and in principle. On the view that matters of moral consequence are to be decided purely according to the predilections of the individual or the local tribe or enclave, there can be no principled basis to oppose the resulting decisions of the majority, including the decision to ignore the wishes of minorities. Why not? Why should I promote anyone's happiness but my own? Why should I honor the "rights" of others? Having affiliated myself with a group whose powers cannot be successfully resisted, why should I do anything beyond my own interests or at variance with my own feelings?

The Marxist wing of utilitarianism surely will not be at a loss to contribute additional self-contradictions in an attempt to answer such questions. As we have learned from this agile quarter, all social reforms and expansion of rights have been hard won from the grudging power elite. However, no more is surrendered than is necessary to keep profits high and business as usual. I offer this rebuttal not because it has any intrinsic merit; less because any Marxist utterance has ever passed a proof test. I offer it as an illustration of the self-refuting nature of materialist-empiricist theories of morals and jurisprudence. Marx himself went wrong when he chose to labor over the psychological materialism of Epicurus for his doctoral dissertation and thus ensured that he would never understand that aching problem of mind that has defeated all materialists. (In both *The Holy Family* and *The German Ideology* he gives just enough attention to the mind/body problem to establish that he didn't understand it.) More important than the ignorance he bequeathed, however, is the fact that, if the Marxist vision of human nature is true, then the Marxist social imperatives are pointless. Once we regard human nature as no more than an especially complex form of purely material organization, totally programmed from without and unswervingly committed to purely material conditions of life, there can be no moral imperative of any sort. "To each according to his needs." Why? "From each according to his ability." Why? What is the principle, and what is its source?

What the nineteenth century happily and aptly called *moral science* is, as Locke recognized, an axiomatic science akin to geometry. It proceeds from first principles (major premises), which are the necessary starting point for moral discourse of any kind. The major premises of moral discourse are always subject to dispute and disagreement and, as universal propositions, can never be confirmed experientially. Political life begins only when certain of these premises are taken to be true, even as the moral philosophers quite properly raise objections. Such rights as persons have are brought into being by these premises and have no existence apart from them. Such rights are, then, the most unnatural entities in the universe, existing as they do only in the realm of moral reasoning and never in the realm of space and time.

The purely historical or social origins of these rights are entirely beside the point. At the risk of surprising the popular Dr. Carl Sagan—who tells us breathlessly in *Cosmos* that (somehow), "hydrogen made us!"—I might say here only that these rights could not have their origins in our genes, our neurons, or (even) hydrogen. Moral imperatives, oughts, and universals do not inhere in matter. Genes are no more "selfish" than they are brave or humorous, and hydrogen no more made us than stones made the Cathedral of Salisbury.[3] Surely some rights have been won in battle, others at court, still others in court. But when (or how) these came about is irrelevant to their nature, which, as I have argued, is propositional, not material or empirical. Inextricably tied to the major premises of an irreducibly moral argument, these rights become relative at the instant we regard their generating premises as relative. If the moral premises are answerable to the sentiments of the masses, the rights must be hostage to the vagaries of popular fancy. In short, there is no way of cutting rights away from their moral roots without eliminating the vitality of both.

It is true that the conclusions reached syllogistically are relative to the truths asserted in the major premise. Thus, telishment is unjust in relation to the premise that *the innocent shall go unpunished*. As noted above, the major premises of moral arguments are debatable, but this actually provides less room for the pluralist than might be expected. The civilized, orderly, and protected life of citizens in a just state is made possible only by the suspension of debate when it comes to certain key propositions of morality—for example, when debate is closed on whether or not suspects ought to be tortured into giving evidence against themselves, whether or not a person's residence ought to be capriciously invaded by government agents, whether or not religious dissenters ought to have their properties confiscated. Purely philosophical arguments can be offered on both sides of such possibilities, but a given political regime is defined according to its unarguable stand on just such matters. Once the decision is made to bring about and to preserve a constitutional order that respects the moral and rational nature of its citizens, any number of major premises and any number of moral-jural conclusions become virtually hardened in stone. Indeed, once the decision is made that a given community will be regulated by law—that actions of a certain sort will be punished when these are judged to arise from the actor's freely chosen options—any number of implicated propositions can no longer be taken as relative. And to live as a citizen within that community is to accept those originating premises and their chain of logical implications. It is here that pluralism ceases and citizenship begins.

III

Many volumes have been devoted to the nature of the so-called social sciences, particularly as these disciplines seek to establish themselves as *scientific*. This is, or course, a very large question grounded in the concepts and technicalities of philosophy of science. For present purposes, the social sciences are confined to psychology, sociology, psychiatry, and the empirical divisions of political science and economics. Why such traditionally humanistic subjects as history and political science now aspire to the status of social sciences is a question that must be ignored here. Without presuming to settle the question of what constitutes a scientific discipline, I should set forth at least some of the more general considerations likely to keep the question alive indefinitely.

Aristotle, in his *Physics* and *Metaphysics*, was the first to attempt a formal classification of scholarship according to the methodologies and the explanatory goals of various disciplines. Many attempts have followed since then, some of them quite in the Aristotelian tradition and others quite opposed to it.

Among the most influential contemporary philosophers of science who may be said to support the Aristotelian classification is Carl Hempel, who has for many years defended what is called the nomological-deductive model of science. According to this model, the essential character of science—any science—is revealed in the logic of its explanations. A science, therefore, is a discipline able to provide scientific explanations. What is distinctive about such explanations is that they are grounded in universal laws answerable to (refutable by) controlled observation. Thus, once we are in possession of Newton's gravitational laws, we are able to explain why objects fall simply by invoking the (universal) laws that cover such events. The forthcoming explanations are framed in terms of laws *(nomos)* such that the events in question are formal deductions from the laws themselves. Thus, *if all bodies attract each other with a force proportional to the product of their masses and inversely proportional to the square of the distance between them*, and *if X is a body*, then *necessarily X must fall*.

Criteria of such stringency must exempt the social sciences from serious consideration as sciences, for none of them is in possession of a single universal law known to be true. Lacking such laws, these disciplines are unable to offer scientific explanations of the nomological-deductive variety and are, therefore, at best merely aspiring sciences.

Critics of the nomological-deductive model have argued that very few scientific disciplines have ever answered to these criteria. Rather, the model, though perhaps apt for classical physics and astronomy, is entirely incompatible with the biological and social sciences or, for that matter, with a modern physics forced to accept the intrinsic uncertainty (probability) of subatomic phenomena. Evolutionary laws, such as natural selection and survival of the fittest, are not predictive in the way required by the nomological-deductive model; that is, given these laws of evolutionary biology, we are still totally unable to predict the elimination or the appearance of specific species. Similarly, because of the Heisenberg principle, the phenomena of the subatomic world cannot ever be explained by recourse to a universal law since the phenomena themselves are determined only on average and not instantaneously.

Without going into details, it is sufficient to note that the social sciences obtain no relief from these challenges to the nomological-deductive criteria of scientific explanation. The social sciences do not even possess the nonpredictive laws of evolutionary biology, let alone the rigidly deterministic laws of classical physics. Furthermore, the phenomena of quantum physics, which defy deterministic formulations, have no known parallel in the social spheres of activity. What plagues the social sciences is not the Heisenbergian uncertainty of quantum effects but the stubborn refusal of human beings to conform to the theoretical dictates of the social scientist! Moreover, such laws as the social sciences have proclaimed are, without exception, either falsified in fact or unfalsifiable in principle. That is, they are either scientifically wrong or scientifically useless. In light of this, it would be far more prudent to refer to these disciplines as social studies, not as social science.

These considerations led a number of influential psychologists (notably B. F. Skinner) to abandon the philosophical debate and to content themselves with nontheoretical and purely observational modes of inquiry and explanation. The recommended approach, which became something of a philosophy of social science, has been that of descriptivism, a modest Baconian affair which, by way of Hume, has come to settle for reliable correlations between precisely controlled features of the environment and measurable aspects of the animal's behavior. Such laws as are yielded by this policy are (and are intended to be) no more than statistical descriptions of observed regularities. Exposed to identical reinforcement contingencies, animals will tend to behave similarly, the homogeneity of their behavior increasing as they are shaped over longer and longer periods. Tested on a variety of species, including the human species, the basic principles of conditioning have held up quite well, although the behavior investigated and shaped has been confined chiefly to such simple operants as bar pressing, key pecking, vocalizations, and so on.

Beyond the "rat lab" the same descriptive approach has been used to study complex social phenomena and the environmental (social) factors regulating human behavior. Impressive quantities of data have been produced, some of them interesting. Like the studies of animal and human conditioning, though with far less predictive power, this research has spawned any number of correlations or trend-lines suggesting how, *on average*, condition X affects behavior Y.

Still another version of descriptivism, but one more closely related to such genuinely scientific disciplines as neurophysiology and biochemistry, is psychobiology (or physiological psychology), in which correlations are obtained between aspects of brain function and aspects of behavior. Again, mountains of fact have resulted from research in this tradition, and we now have a truly impressive catalogue of reliable relations between the neural and the psychological dimensions of animal and human behavior, emotion, and perception.

No universal law has emerged from these three descriptive and correlational fields of research, nor is any one of them in a position to predict reliably what every person will do under a given set of conditioning or social or (even) neurological procedures. In all three fields, predictive efficiency is generally won at the cost of realism.

These assets and liabilities aside, however, the central question to be addressed in the present context is the relevance and applicability of these disciplines to law, to justice, to moral science. We can begin to answer this question by examining how these disciplines are now in fact used within legislative and jural contexts. They are used in such a wide variety of ways, however, that only an illustrative rather than an exhaustive review is possible here. First, there is the exculpatory function served by the social sciences, the function most visible in the area of the infamous insanity defense but pervasive throughout the criminal justice system. Through the peculiar discretionary powers granted to judges and to parole committees, convicted felons often are partially relieved of the burden of their crime on the basis of social factors regarded as causative. They thus are the beneficiaries of a theory of environmental determinism that has never been confirmed even on average and that could not be confirmed by the individual case. If, for example, poverty caused crime—in any scientifically meaningful sense of causation—then all (or nearly all) impoverished persons would commit crimes and the affluent would not. What is ironic about this exculpatory function of the social sciences is that it seeks to justify or pardon certain actions on the basis of just those conditions the law requires rational and moral beings to rise above! If, in fact, there were no poverty, no disappointment, no frustration, no failure, no depression, and no greed, we might well be able to get by without laws of any kind. Thus, to show (or allege) that Smith did what he did "because" he was poor (frustrated, angry, envious, etc.) can be no more than to recount those temptations to wrongful conduct envisaged by the legislation *ab initio*. The conflation here is between explanation and exculpation. It does not follow from the fact (or the allegation) that Smith did X because of Y that Smith deserves to be excused. What would be exculpatory, of course, is proof that Y deprived Smith of all rational alternatives—for example, that Smith did X at gunpoint, or because his degree of retardation prevented him from comprehending the consequences of X, or accidentally. But if Smith produced action X under any of these conditions, then from a moral and jural perspective he did not do X at all. What one does at gunpoint is not a voluntary action for which the actor is morally responsible, nor is what one does when too retarded to form means-ends strategies, or when helplessly victimized by accidental occurrences. *Mens rea* is lacking in all of these instances.

Quite apart from the unreliability of the data compiled by the social sciences is the incompatibility between the premises of justice and the premises of the social sciences. Persons charged with a crime not only are presumed to be innocent but are answerable only for their own conduct. As noted at the beginning of this essay, we abandoned the luxury of phratric justice and group liability in the archonates of Draco and Solon. Thus, it is utterly irrelevant that defendants fall within a given racial or social or economic category as we proceed to determine their guilt and (therefore) their moral responsibility. We would not convict a man of a crime because he is black and because most crimes in his neighborhood are committed by blacks. Being black is not a cause of crime, and thus it cannot excuse a crime. Similarly, neither can poverty, unhappiness, frustration, sibling rivalry, and the like.

In addition to their exculpatory functions, the social sciences have been entrusted with the task of establishing social justifications for legislative and judicial policies. This is evident in a variety of contexts—for example, the findings of psychologists regarding the self-image of black children in segregated schools (*Brown* v. *Board of Education*) and of social scientists regarding the effects of unwanted pregnancies (*Roe* v. *Wade*; *Doe* v. *Bolton*). This mission is, of course, entirely predictable once the courts come to view themselves as social institutions and utilitarianism comes to dominate judicial thinking. Without belaboring the issue, it should be clear that if segregation is wrong, its wrongfulness survives any self-image problem it creates among those who have been segregated; and if abortion is wrong, its wrongfulness survives any social convenience or privilege made possible by abortion. That is, if we take as an unarguable axiom of morals that *the innocent shall go unpunished*—or its extension here to *it is always wrong to take the life of an innocent, nonthreatening human being*—then the position we must take on abortion is uniquely determined by the status accorded to the human fetus. If said fetus is taken not to be a human being, then the social consequences of unwanted pregnancy needn't be argued. But if the fetus is taken to be a human being, such consequences are as irrelevant as they would be to the issue of infanticide or any other homicide. I do not argue the merits of Roe's or Doe's cases here; I only note that social and psychological factors are quite beside the moral point at issue and are incompatible with the formal, rational, and argumentative methods of jurisprudence.

In addition to these exculpatory and justifying functions, the social sciences—the psychosocial point of view—can be seen as having a certain validating function with respect to classes of conduct traditionally regarded as inimical to the best interests of the person and the state. Through their vaunted "value-neutral" descriptions, their counts and polls and dimensionless measures, the social sciences have been apologists for vice, both petty and substantial. Taken collectively, the findings unearthed by them have reinforced the now pervasive fallacy that morality is relative and that, accordingly, there can be no principled basis upon which to constrain the activities of consenting adults, except (perhaps) where serious injury or death is possible. One need only reflect briefly on the following generalizations to appreciate the extent to which this validating function has entered into our national life:

1. Since there is no well-established correlation between a person's sexual preferences and that person's performance as a parent, there is no justification for denying homosexuals the right of parenthood.

2. Since there is no well-established correlation between a person's attraction to pornographic literature and that person's overall performance as a worker, a social peer, and a citizen, there can be no principled ground for restricting the production and distribution of pornographic materials.

3. Research has turned up no uniform mode of political expression, and so whatever the speaker declares to be a political statement—no matter how vile (*Cohen* v. *California*) or pointless—it must be regarded as such within the context of the First Amendment.

4. There is no measurable dimension of human performance that

totally divides the sexes. Therefore, there can be no basis for restricting women or men to any given occupational domain.

No one should be lulled into the belief that the social sciences have merely been messengers of truth, indifferent to the uses to which messages are put. The major professional associations (American Psychological Association, American Psychiatric Association, American Sociological Association) have officially lobbied for all sorts of causes beyond the purely self-serving ones. The American Psychological Association, for example, will not hold its conventions in states that have failed to ratify the Equal Rights Amendment—though it did encourage its members to attend the International Psychology Congress in Leipzig! So-called gay rights coalitions have a special place within such organizations, coalitions which became especially strident at about the time the American Psychiatric Association voted to remove homosexuality from the category of treatable diseases. One or another influential wing of each of these organizations has also been in the vanguard of legislation that would protect the right of minors to obtain birth-control devices and medicines as well as abortions without being burdened by something as paleolithic as parental consent. (Studies "have shown" that today's children are sexually "more advanced" than their predecessors.) Find any cause that is tied to the inflated concept of liberation, and it is likely that the social science community has attached itself to it.

This is not to say that social scientists are prepared to follow their own odd logic in any direction, however. When it comes to findings and mere correlations, we are in possession of some that are far more reliable than those routinely gathered in the laboratory. For example, the one datum that predicts better than any other the probability that a person will commit a felony is the fact that that person has already committed felonies. Were justice to be meted out according to the statistical laws of the social sciences, there would be no reason to conduct trials. Knowing that the defendant had a criminal record, we would be able to predict, with far better than chance-accuracy, that he will commit a crime again. Indeed, we might go so far as to presume that he committed the one he has been charged with, apart from any direct and material evidence to that effect. Similarly, if children are now so different from their historical predecessors, so mature and precocious in the facts of life and the ways of the world, why have the social scientists not agitated to eliminate the special provisions of juvenile justice? And why should the abuse or neglect of children be judged as any more regrettable than the abuse or neglect of adults? And if, as the social scientists continue to inform us, the only significant differences between the sexes arise from the sex-role stereotyping that is part of our childhood conditioning, it must follow that our social dispositions are determined early in life through the agency of adult models. But if this is so, then it must also be the case that homosexual inclinations and dispositions are thus determined and that, therefore, the sexual preferences of a parent will be decisive in the child's formation of such preferences. And if the pregnant child of twelve has a right to make decisions that will affect the balance of her life—and to do so without the approval or even the apprisal of her parents—then why is the same child not prosecutable for the offenses of fornication (where applicable), solicitation (where applicable), or adultery (where applicable)?

In these and related matters, justice is light years ahead of the social sciences. It is recognized by the judicial point of view—in contrast with the psychosocial point of view—that some decisions cannot enjoy the full benefits of rationality until a person has attained a certain ripeness of age and has engaged the complexities of life. More importantly, it recognizes that the rightness or wrongness of an action must be assessed independently of the actor's eagerness to perform it, and independently of the fraction of the populace that might be inclined to favor it. The judicial point of view comprehends that the domain of *oughts* does not exist in merely material nature; that it originates only in beings who could do otherwise and now must be persuaded not to either by the rationality of law or by its threats. The psychosocial point of view, which tends to regard all human activities as determined by whatever means, is thus at variance with the most fundamental principle of justice: the principle of personal responsibility, itself a deduction from the premise of moral autonomy.

It will be argued that all persons are not equally rational; that some persons have especially strong impulses; that others have been so victimized by the force of circumstance as to be stripped of the moral power of self-control; that autonomy is a relative and shifting attribute, enjoyed primarily by those the fates have blessed with privileges; that, because of all this, justice—no matter how noble its origins or ennobling its premises—has all too often been an instrument of oppression, rendering many people far less autonomous and far more compliant with the wishes of an elite class; and finally, that the methods and findings of the social sciences speak directly to just these facts of social history and therefore provide the means by which the hypocrisies of justice might be exposed and eliminated. These are not entirely vacuous arguments, except when they are stretched (as they often are) to absurd conclusions. For example, it is quite true and empirically verifiable that rationality is not uniformly distributed throughout the human race. It is absent in infancy, limited in childhood, and still defective even on the threshold of the teenage years. As with all psychological attributes, rationality displays ontogenetic variations and, in some cases, even downturns very late in life. It can be acutely impoverished by traumas, intoxicants, and disease, and chronically impoverished by genetic and birth defects as well as by severe insults to the central nervous system. Thus, an argument to the effect that all persons cannot be regarded as equally autonomous because all persons are in fact not equally rational is sound so far as it goes. The argument becomes unsound when it implies—from the fact that rationality is distributed in vanishingly small gradations—that personal responsibility, too, is a continuously distributed variable. What is neglected in such an argument is the existence of a threshold beyond which all persons are properly regarded as sufficiently rational to qualify as autonomous for purposes of justice. It matters not that above this threshold criterion of rationality there is still a continuous gradation of the attribute. For all practical (but still judicial) purposes, this threshold criterion may be regarded as satisfied when the very facts of the crime indicate a developed capacity for means-ends strategy. Putting the case tersely, I would say that if all mentally retarded men and women were put behind bars today, the national crime statistics would be totally unaffected. To be able to commit a crime is also to be able not to.

It is also true that certain persons seem to be far more impulsive than others and, in the idiom of social science, to lack impulse control. But from this fact it follows only that such persons should be especially mindful of the penalties of law. In extremely rare cases, the lack of self-control may be so total as to yield what in ancient Roman law was called the *fanaticus* and what in Elizabethan law was designated the *wild beast*.[4] Rome was disposed to execute, exile, or enslave such beings on the grounds that they did not qualify as (rational) *human* beings. In such cases, there is no need for the expertise of the social scientist, for everyone will quickly recognize the defendant as a nonrational entity. Again, the very facts of the crime and of the defendant's comportment provide grounds for exoneration. The basic considerations were well known to jurists long before the humbug of psychiatry. As early as 1723, in the famous British trials of Edward Arnold, Justice Tracy charged the jury thus:

> Every man that so departs from reason, every wicked man may be said to be a madman; but I hope that shall not skreen all that so act, and free and exempt them from punishment. . . . If a man be deprived of his reason, and consequently his intention, he cannot be guilty . . . punishment is intended for example, and to deter other persons from wicked designs, but the punishment of a madman, a person that hath no design, can have no example. This is on the one side. On the other side, we must be very cautious; it is not every idle humour of a man that will exempt him from justice . . . it must be a man that is totally deprived of his understanding and memory, and that doth not know what he is doing, no more than an infant, than a brute, or a wild beast.[5]

If we are concerned with "every idle humour," the social sciences may be consulted. But the jury can recognize "an infant . . . a brute . . . a wild beast" without the benefit of psychosocial speculations.

It appears to be a law of life that some persons will come to enjoy privileges and that others will be bent by the force of circumstance, often as a result of nothing ascribable to the persons themselves. But the lottery of life cannot be used as a warrant for suspended reason or a license for criminality. From the fact that one's social or economic standing is relative to the standing of others, it does not follow that one's autonomy is relative; just as, from the fact that some are better chess players than others, it does not follow that poorer players are not free to make their moves and, indeed, to improve their game. To the extent that privileged persons have used (perverted) justice to wrongful ends, such persons are blameworthy and punishable. The remedy for venality is not its proliferation but its extinction. If it is wrong to suspend justice for the rich, it is wrong to suspend it for the poor.

At last we come to a legitimate function for the social sciences: exposing or helping to expose certain injudicious trends in the law. It is here that the purely descriptive and correlational methods of the social sciences are most useful, for it is here that we are interested not in developing and articulating basic moral-jural reasoning but in determining whether the fruits of this reasoning have flourished *in practice*. A study that shows, for example, that the probability of a death sentence for the crime of rape is eighteen times greater for blacks who have raped white women than for whites who have raped black women virtually establishes the fact of judicial capriciousness, bias, and malfeasance. There is a need and ample room for studies of judicial procedure and judicial outcomes, studies by which the nation may assess the extent to which its moral ends are served by its judicial means. The same useful function is served by specialties within the social sciences able to develop and interpret tests of mental competence or of the accuracy of eyewitness reports, or really of any of a large number of purely factual assessments that may bear upon the process of adjudication. Justice may make use of the facts of social science without borrowing its generally defective moral or quasi-moral conclusions, and without ever entering that loud arena of theoretical frenzy in which the social scientist spends far too much time.

IV

The concept of justice is inextricably and formally tied to the concept of moral autonomy. It arises from the premise that beings regarded as answerable to and protected by the obligations of law are rational and are free in the moral sense. A law or a pattern of laws at variance with the conclusions of rationality and indifferent to the moral implications of human autonomy is self-refuting and ultimately indefensible. Thus, the promises of law must be at one with the premises of law. The overarching promise is that persons who organize their conduct in a rational way and who seek to live their lives in a manner that respects the irreducibly moral standing of other human beings will be protected by law.

The premises of law are, in the last analysis, moral premises and are philosophically arguable, within limits—the limits set by that presumption of moral autonomy necessary for there to be law in the first instance. Once certain basic premises are granted, such that the political state may be said to exist, the more fundamental conclusions of law follow by implication and entailment. In this respect the logic of jurisprudence is properly indifferent to such variables as popular tastes, enthusiasms, desires, and impulses. We may say, then, that the logic of jurisprudence is specifically indifferent to what is relative.

The methods and findings of the social sciences are incompatible with the axiomatic character of jurisprudence and are incapable of illuminating that realm of universal propositions within which the just state must find its moorings. Whatever refinements the institution of justice may undergo are the gifts of moral science, not of social science or any other purely descriptive enterprise. The bare facts of the material world contain neither the good nor the bad, the should nor the shouldn't, a right nor a duty. Thus, no description of the bare facts of the material world, no matter how complete or precise, can address these moral entities which arise from rational discourse on subjects of moral consequence. Such rights as this discourse yields do not occur in nature and are thus not natural; they are sublime, and it is the task of civilization to keep them so.

Notes

1. For lengthier treatments of these trends, consult my *An Intellectual History of Psychology* (New York: Macmillan, 1976) and *Toward a Science of Human Nature: Essays on the Psychologies of Hegel, Mill, Wundt, and James* (New York: Columbia University Press, 1982).
2. A fuller discussion of this can be found in chapter 1 of my *Psychology and Law: Can Justice Survive the Social Sciences?* (New York: Oxford University Press, 1979).
3. On the failure of evolutionary materialism to account for the established facts of human psychology, see the last chapter of my *Systems of Modern Psychology: A Critical Sketch* (New York: Columbia University Press, 1979).
4. The categories of *furiosus* and *fanaticus* in ancient Roman law are akin to what in postclassical times was referred to as "the raving, raging lunatic."
5. Arnold, 16 *Howell's State Trials* 695.

Reason, Anger, and Retribution

JEFFREY LEIGH SEDGWICK

The retributive model of punishment has returned to respectability of late even among academicians and scholars. Not so long ago, it was de rigueur in educated circles to declare that punishment is itself a crime, nothing more than "an irrational zeal for inflicting pain upon one who has inflicted pain (or harm or loss)."[1] It was argued that society could profitably abandon its fixation with punishment (or vengeance, since many scholars seem to have confused the two) in favor of either rehabilitation, by which the offender is diagnosed and the "illness" cured, or social intervention, whereby social conditions causing crime are identified and altered.[2]

Scholarly fascination with both rehabilitation and social intervention has waned, due in part to the demonstrated lack of success in rehabilitating offenders and in part to the arbitrary exercise of power by correctional officials whose activities are cloaked behind a benign medical metaphor for their role. Further, the causes of crime have been found to be remarkably intractable to social manipulation; and the propriety of a causal understanding of crime has itself been called into question.[3] Consequently, retribution and retributive theories of punishment are enjoying something of a renaissance.

One of the more interesting aspects of the current revival of retributive theories is the appearance of a division among retributivists, reflected in the essays by Daniel Robinson and Walter Berns. At issue is the nature and role of anger in punishment and criminal justice. On the one hand are retributivists such as Robinson who argue that law and criminal justice should respond only to the criminal act, not to the affective components or reactions of citizens to the act and its consequences. On the other hand, some retributivists, like Berns, justify their position on the ground that punishment and criminal justice must acknowledge anger since "anger is the unique human passion that leads us to cry out for justice."[4]

At root, this disagreement among retributivists reflects two very different understandings of ethics and moral philosophy. Those rejecting the relevance of anger to a discussion of punishment typically ground their arguments in the Kantian theory of ethics and morality. As will be shown, such a Kantian approach to morals emphasizes an ethic of intentionality or will. Retributivists stressing anger are more likely grounded in Aristotelian ethics, which modify the ethics of intentionality with an ethic of consequences. Whereas the Kantian position hinges on the dichotomy between reason (or mind) and passion (or body), the Aristotelian position depends on a tripartite division of the human soul into reason, spirit (or *thymos*), and desire.

Since citizens, or humans living in political communities, have both minds and bodies, it would appear that politics and justice must somehow mediate between reason and desire. Aristotle understood this mediation to involve the cultivation and activation of *thymos* or spiritedness; further, he understood that *thymos* or spiritedness would behold injustice with anger. Consequently, justice would inevitably need to be conversant with anger.

In order to understand this issue more fully and its implications for a retributive theory of punishment, it is necessary to consider both the Kantian and Aristotelian theories of ethics and their respective abilities to support criminal justice in a political community.

I. Reason and Kant's Ethic of Intentionality

The clearest statement of the retributive argument based on reason alone is found in the writings of Immanuel Kant. The distinctive contribution of Kant to political philosophy is that he was the first political philosopher to argue that moral duty for its own sake is the highest human good. In *The Republic*, Socrates showed Glaucon that it is the contemplative life which is choiceworthy for itself, not the moral life. And the Platonic dialogues argued that morality is necessary for human happiness properly understood. Thus, morality serves man's natural end. Kant's understanding of nature, however, differed so fundamentally from that of the ancients that he was led to conclude that nature must be overcome in the name of morality.

Kant's approach to the question of moral duty can be understood best in light of both Rousseau's and Hume's philosophies. Kant learned from Rousseau to respect the common man and to subordinate intellectual pursuits, such as cultivation of the arts and sciences, to moral duty. Rousseau demonstrated an unresolved tension between natural duties and science; he resolved this tension through the device of the general will, which was confined within national boundaries and which elevated the moral life above science. Kant goes beyond generalization within national boundaries (that is, he goes beyond the Rousseauian general will) to stress the universalization of moral precepts. In so doing, he derives duty from right by a purer and more formal process than Rousseau had relied upon.

Hume's influence on Kant was in leading him to question the cognitive status of all inferences about causation. Kant read Hume to say that science, insofar as it is grounded in observation of behavior, is based upon unsubstantiated opinions about causal relationships. All scientific laws are synthetic constructs of the mind. More particularly, since synthetic constructs may be either a priori or a posteriori, science rests on unsubstantiated, synthetic, a priori constructs.

Kant's understanding of Hume led him to conclude that traditional concepts of natural order or right were irrelevant. The natural essence of things cannot be known by the human mind. Rather, the human mind synthesizes a priori about phenomenal things. Thus, man is fundamentally free from nature; in his freedom, man orders his existence by synthesizing rules or postulates about existence. The phenomenal world, the world of fact, is thus independent of the noumenal world of morality and the *ought*. The noumenal world is not derived from what is; rather, it is derived from man's freedom to synthesize.

Perhaps the most accessible treatment of Kantian ethics is found in his *Foundations of the Metaphysics of Morals*, the purpose of which is to establish that morality is indeed possible.[5] Kant does not, in the *Foundations*, disagree with earlier formulations of what is moral (that is, the content of morality) but rather disagrees with the formal process by which morality is traditionally defined. Typically, morality is supported by reference to religion or theories about the nature of man. But Kant wished to defend morality independent of both experience and religious dogma. His beginning point is thus the phenomenon of the moral person; he then reasons about the premises of such a being and judges whether these premises are acceptable.

The first section of the *Foundations of the Metaphysics of Morals* begins with the assertion that nothing is an unqualified good except a good will.[6] One should notice in this formulation the total emphasis on intent rather than on result or consequence. Kant takes issue with classical formulations of the four virtues (wisdom, courage, temperance or moderation, and justice), none of which was unqualifiedly superior to the others. However, Kant criticizes only the first three virtues as being insufficient. He does not claim justice to be incomplete.

The ancients, especially Plato and Aristotle, believed in the superiority of wisdom and philosophy over practical life and politics. Also, the ancients looked to actions and not intents. In *The Nicomachean Ethics* Aristotle states, like Kant, that intents are rarely seen in the world.[7] Aristotle thus judges by the visible actions and consequences. But the resulting standard is inherently inegalitarian, for not all have the capacity to act well. Kant, however, looks to intent or will. Presumably all have an equal capacity to intend to do good; thus, Kant's standard emphasizes an equal respect for all as willing characters.

Kant next considers whether happiness is the human end. He suggests that if it were, nature would have endowed mankind with trustworthy instincts to guide the way to happiness. But instead of trustworthy instincts, mankind is endowed with reason. From this fact, the ancients inferred that the contemplative life is the happiest; Kant, however, rejects the contemplative life because it ignores both will and human action. The fact of reason joined to will points Kant toward some notion of reasoned willing as the human good and away from happiness and contemplation as human ends.

Yet what is proper reasoned willing? Is man to act from inclination? Kant replies no, for individuals are not praised for doing that which they are inclined to do. Kant supposes that duty is acting to overcome all inclination in favor of respecting the moral law. For example, we esteem or honor citizens only when their inclinations point away from the call of duty and yet they act according to duty. Kant believes that the important characteristic of duty is that it is ignorant of all particulars and takes its guidance from pure form. Hence it must be a priori or prior to all experience and knowledge of particulars.[8]

Kant concludes the first section of the *Foundations* by claiming that the common man's opinion of morality is correct: only willing in accordance with the moral law irrespective of particular consequences is laudable or praiseworthy. The only difficulty is that citizens are concerned with happiness as well as with moral duty. Hence the need is to demonstrate that obedience to duty is the human end (or source of purest happiness); this, for Kant, requires only a clarification of common opinion on moral matters and not a fundamental change or redirection.

The second section of the *Foundations* begins with a vigorous attack on those who attempt empirical proofs or defenses of morality. Kant argues that duty originates in human reasoning about what it means to be a rational being. This again is a priori or independent of experience of particulars. Kant notes that only rational beings are capable of acting on principles or conceptions of law, and this capacity he calls will or practical reason. Now if reason alone is capable of simply determining the will, then objective conditions (those which reason formally determines to be necessary) coincide with subjective conditions (incentives or considerations of consequences to which our inclinations either attract or repel us). But where reason alone cannot command the will, then duty operates to constrain the imperfect will. Kant willingly accepts that "the actual case of man" is that "will is not of itself in complete accord with reason"; consequently, men are both open to and in need of the constraint of moral duty.[9]

Kant then introduces the notion of an *imperative*, a command of the reason (based on a conception of principle) to an imperfectly reasoned will in need of constraint. An imperative commands a practical good; a practical good, in turn, "is what determines the will by means of the conception of reason and hence not by subjective causes but, rather, objectively, i.e., on grounds which are valid for every rational being as such. It is distinguished from the pleasant as that which has an influence on the will only by means of a sensation from merely subjective causes, which hold only for the senses of this or that person and not as a principle of reason which holds for everyone."[10] An imperative which commands a practical good and which holds for all rational beings is called a categorical imperative. Such categorical imperatives hold at all times regardless of circumstances. By way of contrast, an imperative which is conditional—either on temporal factors or on phenomenal circumstances—Kant refers to as a hypothetical imperative.

Kant's categorical imperative is to act so that one can, at the same time, will that what he does should become a universal law. In so defining the categorical imperative, Kant attempts to make the formulation of moral law almost trivial. Aristotle, by way of contrast, claimed that the moral was a mean between excess and defect which could be determined only by reference to the particulars of each case. The judgment of these particulars is terrifically difficult because all men and all actions are not equally worthy. Whereas the moderns typically conceive of all citizens as fundamentally equal in the most important respects, the ancients suggested that there were gradations among citizens in both reason and prudence and that these two qualities are inextricably linked to consideration of moral worth. Aristotle, for example, observed the common respect of citizens for morality (though they might differ on its exact definition). But he also acknowledged that some are moral only from fear of punishment and others are moral from love of morality itself (still others are moral as an incidental byproduct of their love of wisdom or truth).

For Kant's formulation of the categorical imperative to be persuasive, he must demonstrate the existence of an objective (that is, formal, rational, and principled) end for every human as a willing or rational creature. To begin, Kant distinguishes objective ends belonging to a class of beings from subjective ends belonging to individual wills. He then argues that the fact of subjective ends held by individual wills points to a common agreement on the importance of each human being acting as a rational, willing individual. In making this point, Kant deliberately abstracts from the particularity of subjective ends (or inclinations) to which individual wills find themselves inclined. Indeed, he stresses the point that:

> in morals, the proper and inestimable worth of an absolutely good will consists precisely in the freedom of the principle of action from all influences from contingent grounds which only experience can furnish. We cannot too much or too often warn against the lax or even base manner of thought which seeks principles among empirical motives and laws, for human reason in its weariness is glad to rest on this pillow. In a dream of sweet illusions (in which it embraces not Juno but a cloud), it substitutes for morality a bastard patched up from limbs of a very different parentage, which looks like anything one wishes to see in it, but not like virtue to anyone who has ever beheld her in her true form.[11]

Once subjective will is abstracted from the particular consequences to which it finds itself inclined, one is left with the pure will free to direct itself as it chooses. This pure will, abstractly conceived of as volition, is that upon which moral responsibility (and praise and blame) is premised. Further, such pure will is an end in itself and is considered such by all rational, willing beings.[12] The will does not exist for any other thing; it is not a means to an end external to the rational human being.

Thus, the categorical imperative commands us that one "act so that you treat humanity, whether in your own person or in that of another, always as an end and never as a means only."[13] This categorical imperative is grounded in an objective end or natural standard which is not outside of man but rather inheres in man as a reasoned, willing being. If man had a natural end outside of himself, then man's will would be unfree or determined and moral responsibility would be impossible. Moral responsibility is premised on the possibility of a will, as an end in itself, open to the call of duty. Indeed, the fact of willing by human beings leads to the elevation of moral duty to the highest good, since willing is not for the sake of anything exterior to man. Rather, duty is good for itself just as willing is unique and common to all men. Duty is the objective end belonging to the class of beings we call humans.

Kant's formulation of duty as the objective end of all humans fundamentally frees human will from the constraints of either natural law or religious canon. The absence of such vertical controls over human will suggests a need for horizontal controls among humans. The horizontal control Kant relies on is respect for others' dignity and reasoned willing. This horizontal control, or duty, is derived from the definition of man as a willing being whose will is complete and an end in itself.

The final section of the *Foundations* tries to prove that the categorical imperative is indeed a fact. In the first two sections of the book, Kant has described the categorical imperative and established the meaning of morality (by examining the premises upon which the moral being acts). Kant considers moral duty or practical reason to be the highest good. Theoretical reason, by way of contrast, is of value chiefly in pointing out its own limits and hence the superiority of moral reasoning. Kant defines theoretical reason as a projection of the human mind which attempts to explain the phenomenal world by postulating natural laws of causality. Moral or practical reasoning is independent of theoretical reason, since it is derived from reasoned will itself and since theoretical reason cannot explain morality. The noumenal world, concerned as it is with *oughts*, is quite literally invisible to theoretical science or reason. Consequently, theoretical and practical (or moral) reason are disjoint, and therefore theoretical reason can neither explain nor challenge practical reason. Practical reason stands alone and supreme. This independence and supremacy presents, however, a grave political difficulty, for political communities contain both moral principles and particular phenomena such as actions. On Kant's formulation, neither of these can know or be conversant with the other.

But surely theoretical reason and practical reason must somehow be reconciled, since humans are moral beings with bodies. The actions of humans are phenomenal or observable and consequently subject to universal laws.[14] Kant's attempt to reconcile the phenomena of human action with the proposition that moral duty is the highest human good takes the form of a particular philosophy of history. Typically, a philosophy of history argues that nature has an end independent of man's action and that history is a gradual unfolding of human life toward this end. Kant must reject any such philosophy in order to maintain moral duty as the highest human end. But Kant does need a philosophy of history which explains human actions in a way that makes morality possible. More specifically, it must be shown that human actions, which tend toward happiness or pleasure, are led to accept moral duty. Kant's philosophy of history must make morality and moral duty possible without making the free choices of the moral being unnecessary.

Kant's philosophy of history is predicated on a distinction between human history and the "history of bees and beavers." Human history is distinct in that humans have reason; their actions are not wholly determined by instinct, as are the actions of brutes and animals. Now man is by nature reasonable, yet nature does not contain a firm plan for the human race which reason can discern. Rather, that plan emerges out of the spontaneous and unlimited exercise of reason. Nature thus points beyond itself toward some plan that reason, not history, will articulate.

Kant argues that nature works not through moral duty (which emanates from the reasoned will) but rather through selfish desires. This working of history through selfish desire is satisfactory for Kant because the end result of nature's work is wholly unproblematic—that is, nature is working its way toward the achievement of a universal civic society which is an unqualified good.[15] In this universal civic society, the law is neutral between vice and virtue; consequently, both moral and immoral men can live together in this community.

The law is neutral between vice and virtue because its aim is elsewhere. Kant characterizes man as unsocially sociable: "Man has an inclination to associate with others, because in society he feels himself to be more than a man, i.e., as more than the developed form of his natural capacities. But he also has a strong propensity to isolate himself from others, because he finds in himself at the same time the unsocial characteristic of wishing to have everything go according to his own wish."[16] The antagonism among humans, each wishing to have his own way, propels mankind into civil society where law restrains the most aggressive tendencies of each person. Selfishness, to put it another way, drives mankind into political communities where law regulates the passionate desires. And the law's restraint of passionate desires constitutes the condition under which freedom to act can flourish. Hence, all types of men with all types of desires are thrust into civil society for the sake of freedom and security.

Kant's formulation of moral virtue as universalization means that all humans have a capacity for morality which cannot be coerced by the law or by particular habits of behavior cultivated by the law. Rather, morality is a product of human will in a condition of unrestrained freedom. Freedom, in turn, requires law and civil society. The law of such a civil society aims at universalization, freedom, and generality—the conditions of morality. And finally, within this context, the human will may develop into a good will. Notice, in all of this, the peculiar philosophy of history: human behavior, which is phenomenal and hence subject to laws of causality amenable to theoretical reasoning, is reconciled with the proposition that moral duty or practical reason is supreme by the argument that history brings about the conditions of morality but is impotent with regard to actually establishing the good will.

To a substantial degree, Kant's thinking undergirds contemporary liberalism in its understanding of law and morality, particularly the beliefs that all humans have an equal capacity for morality, that law cannot coerce morality, that the law properly aims at generality and universality, and that society is responsible for establishing material conditions within which freedom can exist. Indeed, far from being an ivory-tower exercise in obscure theorizing, an investigation of Kant's moral philosophy illuminates key aspects of the way in which liberal democracies define themselves and their criminal justice systems.

Yet a nagging problem remains. Earlier it was said that Kant's distinction between theoretical reason and practical reason is problematic for politics, since political communities contain moral actors or, more specifically, reasoned wills and bodies. Kant tries to reconcile the noumenal world with the phenomenal world, as any political community must, through the device of a universal history. Yet his essay on the idea of a universal history closes with an unsubtle hint that the necessary reconciliation is uncertain. Kant's final appeal in that essay is to arouse the desire for fame among statesmen by arguing that morality is the only path to fame. This final appeal indicates that politics and morality (or practical reason) are not coextensive and ultimately may not converge without resort to utilitarian arguments about ambition and glory. Kant's metaphysics of morals leaves an amoral politics and an apolitical morality. The consequence is that human beings, pursuing happiness through politics, never come to achieve morality. One might then well ask, what is the good of Kant's morality?

II. Intention, Consequence, and Anger

Kant's metaphysics of morals leaves an unresolved tension between moral duty and politics. Indeed, it is unclear from Kant's presentation whether concern for morality can be brought successfully into the everyday life of political communities. This problem is in striking contrast to Aristotle's formulation of ethics, since Aristotle claims at the end of *The Nicomachean Ethics* that this work is equivalent to the *Politics*. More specifically, he says that the *Ethics* is but the first part of the *Politics*, an introduction of sorts.[17] Both politics and ethics, it would appear, concern ends and such honorable things as moral virtue, justice, and nobility.

The Nicomachean Ethics begins with an observation Aristotle shares with Kant. Both thinkers acknowledge that humans act with some end in mind; hence both distinguish between simple, random movement and end-directed activity. Having established that distinction, Aristotle turns to the search for a hierarchy of ends which allows one to order or connect all motions. Without such an order, humans would appear to pursue simple, unconnected pleasures; the resulting behavior is simple hedonism.

Early in his search for the hierarchy of ends, Aristotle enters into a digression on "things beautiful . . . and just." In the course of this digression, he identifies political science as concerned with the beautiful and the just and notes that politics is the architectonic science which orders the practice of all other arts and sciences. Aristotle is concerned with the *what* of ethics, not the *why*. Consequently, a discussion of ethics can take place only among individuals who already accept the need for ethical virtues. A discussion of the *why* of virtue inevitably leads to the causes of virtue which are not themselves virtuous. It seems that whenever the phenomenon of the moral actor is discussed along with the causes of his morality, the phenomenon is inevitably reduced to its causes. If this is true, then no description of morality or the moral actor can take into account the cause of morality without morality or virtue slipping from view. Aristotle's task, then, is to try to make the observed fact of virtue understandable by itself without reference to its causes.

Experience in living brings with it a certain habituation to abiding by the law and the law's commands to act virtuously and justly. Aristotle thus presents morality as emanating initially from habits of action cultivated by law. But then laws, or more particularly legislators, need guidance or direction so that they may accurately command the good for citizens. The knowledge which would guide legislation must be of a practical sort, and it must aim at a practical good which the law could command. One is thus presented with two distinct questions: what is the definition of the good for man; and what is the source of such knowledge—the city's habitual morality, theoretical reasoning, or divine revelation?

Aristotle notes that common opinion holds three different notions of what constitutes human goodness or felicity: wealth, honor, and contemplation. He examines only the first two, finding each to be wanting because neither is sought for its own sake: wealth is useful for the sake of something else which money can buy, and honor is sought as a sign that the honored one is virtuous. Consequently, the reader is left with virtue and contemplation as possible definitions of the good.

Curiously, Aristotle never does thematically discuss the claim of the contemplative life to be the highest or happiest life. Indeed, in both *The Nicomachean Ethics* and the *Politics*, Aristotle seems to be protecting a naively held morality from a wrongly understood Platonic conception of the superiority of the contemplative life. In both the *Ethics* and the *Politics*, knowledge of the whole is dismissed in favor of knowledge of man as the basis of nobility and justice. By obscuring the claim of contemplation to be the good, Aristotle protects the dignity of the knowledge or outlook of the moral actor.

Book Two of the *Ethics* examines virtue and its claim to be the human good. Aristotle claimed in Book One that virtue is the proper working of the human soul. And he deduced from that which is unique to man that the proper working of the soul is its obedience to reason.[18] This deduction from human uniqueness or nature in turn supports the habitual deference to morality which rests on common sense and is a product of civic laws.

Aristotle's political science is the necessary center of study of the human good, since politics claims to know the good (the noble and the just) in constructing laws to promote morality. The central difficulty politics confronts is that, according to Aristotle, not all citizens have an equal capacity or inclination for morality or moral virtue. Morality is cultivated (or commanded) by the law, but this cultivation requires the art or skill of the legislator to guide it—to manipulate pleasure and pain, praise and blame, or reward and punishment in order to inculcate moral virtue.

This initial formulation of the relationship between ethics and politics is problematic on two counts. First, the cause of moral virtue is said to be the same as its corruption: the attraction to pleasures. And second, if moral virtue is a habit acquired through the doing of deeds which the law commands, why does one need moral virtue at all? Why is not the doing of the deed at the behest of a hedonistic calculation sufficient? Aristotle counters these challenges by ascribing moral virtue not simply to the habitual act but also to the choice by the actor to conduct himself in a virtuous manner. In this revised presentation, moral desert or virtue is predicated on acting knowingly, with deliberate choice and with "a firm and immutable disposition of mind."[19]

The role of law is to create habits of action or customs that mold personal character or disposition. Yet character or disposition is incomplete to sustain moral virtue, for character is the product of the legislator's manipulation of pleasures and pains. Choice and knowledge must be added to passion or the desire for pleasure in order to establish moral virtue. Virtue, which is both cultivated through habits and conversant with pleasure and pain, needs to be guided by reason. This is the basis of choice.

What does one need knowledge of in order to choose well and hence to be honorable or praiseworthy? Aristotle claims that the virtues are each means between excess and defect, yet these means are determined not in isolation or abstractly but rather in a particular context and with reference to man.[20] From this it would appear that the knowledge necessary for moral virtue is of two parts: a certain practical knowledge born of dealing with everyday experience, and knowledge of man and especially the good or deserving man.

Aristotle's reminder that virtue includes not only habit but also choice sets the stage for the transition from Book Two of the *Ethics* to Book Three. Whereas Book Two presented moral virtue as existing in the habituation to choosing the virtuous deed, Book Three investigates choice by examining the distinction between voluntary and involuntary actions. Involuntary actions are said to be made through either compulsion or ignorance. The class of actions considered involuntary is small, however; Aristotle defines compulsion and ignorance quite restrictively. For example, he defines compulsion to mean that the principle of action is external to the person and that the person himself contributes nothing to the act. If a tyrant commands us to act in a particular way under threat of dire consequences if we refuse, the action is voluntary because the principle of seeking felicity and avoiding pain is in us and we are the agents of the resulting action. The first component of responsibility is thus that the individual is the agent of the action and is acting on an internal principle. This is an extraordinarily rigorous standard, since in virtually any action we are ourselves the agents of action.

The second component of moral responsibility is said to be knowledge of the consequences of our actions. Where one could know the particulars of his actions, he is responsible. This notion of knowledge is much different from that which would require knowledge of the ends for which one acts. Significantly, Aristotle's definition of knowledge does not excuse actions motivated by passion; such an actor is still morally responsible since, though he cannot understand ends (being under the sway of passionate urges), he can understand the particulars of his passionate actions. This orientation to knowledge and the need of moral responsibility to encompass passionate acts is necessary if morality is to be a useful concept for the bulk of mankind.

Aristotelian morality sees an action and inquires into its causes. Hence this morality must encompass passionate actions, since some men act on simple impulse. Aristotle argues that where a person is the agent of the action, acting on an internal principle, and where that person could know the particulars of his act, then the actor is responsible for the consequences of his action. Yet this understanding is not fully sufficient, for judgment cannot be made solely on the basis of consequences unless chance or fortune is eliminated. So long as chance is a possibility, so long as the unforeseeable circumstance leads to consequences which we did not intend when we acted, what we intended as well as the consequences of our actions must be considered in determining moral desert.

Aristotle's presentation of moral responsibility suggests that responsibility rests in voluntary choice. His discussion never clearly and precisely defines choice except to say that choice is preceded by deliberation and requires some reason or knowledge. Deliberation, in turn, cannot be about either chance events or mathematical certainties. Deliberation takes place only about things which we can affect and hence could potentially be responsible for.

Also, deliberation considers the means in an end-means relationship since means are within our power. Deliberation takes the end as a given, derives the means, and eventually reaches to the first cause of action—the actor. Morality so conceived is concerned with the choice of things we can do, proceeding from a given end to the possible means. The choice of ends seems, on this reading, wholly outside of morality. Now the problem is that in some sense praise and blame rest not only on the choice of appropriate means but also on the willful component of humans which chooses the ends of our actions.

By focusing on actions and choices, Aristotle tries to protect the notion of moral responsibility. Blameworthiness, for example, is said to reflect a bad character; bad character, in turn, is derived from a habit of choosing poorly. But if morality is connected with the choice of ends, then all men who lack knowledge of the best ends must be absolved of responsibility; and morality must be connected to a capacity, wisdom or intellect, which is fundamentally a gift and not a matter of choice. Morality thus would contain a fundamentally amoral component.

By connecting morality only to actions and not to ends, Aristotle assures that humans will be responsible because they can in some sense control their actions (at least more than they can control their wisdom). Yet by excluding the end from morality, Aristotle threatens to propose simple moral relativism. His moral philosophy supposes that we must adhere to the ends given to us regardless of what they are. Aristotle seeks to escape the relativistic implications of his concentration on actions by establishing a standard or measure of ends which would allow one to identify the good. But this perception of the good which leads the good man to will must itself have a source. Aristotle offers two alternative sources: either the end willed by the good man is partly natural and partly manmade, or the end is entirely naturally determined. In the former case, there is and can be no universal basis for understanding morality—different people will construct the end differently. In the latter case, morality (insofar as it is to be useful) must lower its horizons and concern itself only with actions. To the extent morality concerns itself with naturally determined ends, it points to the man who by nature is able to perceive the best or the good. Yet this person is not moral since he is not responsible for his perception of the good. To the extent that morality is to be useful, its amoral component must be hidden from view. Aristotle does this by making morality concerned with actions.

Book Three concludes with a discussion of the eleven virtues which continues throughout Book Four and into Book Five. Aristotle's list of eleven virtues is notable on two counts. First, it is unclear where these eleven virtues come from; in the *Republic,* Plato deduced his four virtues from the parts of the human soul. Aristotle does not similarly deduce his eleven virtues (courage, temperance, liberality, magnificence, magnanimity, proper ambition, mildness in anger, friendship, veracity, facetiousness, and justice). The second notable feature of the list is that Aristotle says there are two "peaks" or preeminent virtues on the list, magnanimity and justice. Magnanimity is said to be the crown or ornament of all the virtues, while justice is said to include all the virtues especially as they are practiced towards others.[21]

In revealing those two peak virtues, Aristotle notes a certain degree of tension between them. To the degree that a citizen is just, he will be courageous since courage is useful for the city. But if the citizen is magnanimous, it is doubtful whether he will be courageous for the city. Indeed, the magnanimous citizen is of questionable value to the city—he will rise so far above his fellows as to be contemptuous of their honors. Rather, he will seek the company only of a few good friends. In this discussion, justice is presented as concerning our behavior toward others; that is, justice is an other-regarding virtue. It concerns exchanges among citizens. Magnanimity, on the other hand, appears to be self-regarding.

The tension between the peak virtues of magnanimity and justice calls into question Aristotle's claim that justice and virtue are coextensive. One might also say that the apparent tension threatens the claim that the *Ethics* and the *Politics* are equivalent in their teachings. Aristotle's discussion of justice is useful here in illustrating how he reconciles virtue and politics. He notes that two things are called unjust: breaking the law and taking more than we deserve. He also distinguishes between partial and universal justice: partial justice is said to be changeable, while universal justice is obeying the law since law (including both custom and religious canon) ordains with respect to all the virtues and vices.

However, the law seems to deal only with the lower virtues such as courage, temperance, and liberality and ignores the social virtues of friendship, veracity, and so on. Though law seems to command only the lower virtues, it is still necessary in order to cultivate certain habits. Law also restrains in useful ways since citizens would not make into law certain extreme atrocities. Consequently, a lawful tyranny would be better than a lawless tyranny where there is no habitual barrier to atrocity.

The standard for legal justice is partial or changeable justice which can be divided into two parts, distributive and commutative (or corrective) justice. In his mathematically precise discussion of justice, Aristotle speaks of the distribution of honors, useful things, and other things. The necessary imprecision of political science, which Aristotle notes time and again in the *Ethics*, thus must come in the determination of the value of each citizen. He notes that the law looks only to the act, not to the individuals involved or their intentions. Indeed, the law takes for granted the value of each citizen. But this is, in politics, the most important question and the question on which regimes differ. It is also the question underlying the other meaning of justice: taking what one deserves.

It is necessary for the judge to correct the law's fundamentally democratic bias by taking intention and individual worth into account. While the act before the law is the same whether a rich person or a poor person was the instigator, it is the judge's responsibility to add consideration of intent and personal worth. In this discussion, the law is seen as only accidentally just and in need of correction by the judge's administration of equity. But what is equity? Is equity a perfection of the law's weakness according to the will of the legislator, and hence simply a means of rectifying the weakness of law (that is, its generality) as a tool?

Or is equity a perfection of the particular legal justice of the realm by the application of a superior type of justice?

If equity is merely a means of correcting for the generality of the law, then one is still left with the problem that the law commands only the lower virtues and ignores the social virtues grounded in judgment. If equity is the perfection of legal justice by application of some superior notion of justice or virtue, then by what understanding is equity guided? It appears that Aristotle believes equity to be superior to legal justice and that he defines equity in light of a more perfect community than the political community, that community being friendship. Friendship is a more perfect association because it calls men to be both magnanimous (self-regarding or proud) and just (other-regarding) at once. Friendship thus combines the two peaks of virtue as the city cannot; additionally, friendship is choiceworthy for its own sake. This makes the whole of virtue choiceworthy as a means to achieving friendship, something which is intrinsically pleasurable.

But if friendship is to guide equity, what can one make of the fact that even good friends are sometimes overcome by passion or desire without intending to do wrong or be immoral? This possibility leads Aristotle to consider continence and incontinence. One way of distinguishing between them is to say that the continent person can overcome his desires while the incontinent, knowing what is right, does something else through the attraction of desire. Another way of making the point would be to say that the incontinent person derives his knowledge of particulars from sense impressions and hence does not act from first principle. In fact, all humans act on a knowledge of particulars, yet the source of this knowledge is important. Some do not deliberate at all, some deliberate on the basis of sense impressions, and others moderate the sensual awareness of particulars with reason.

Interestingly, in his discussion of continence and incontinence, Aristotle specifically distinguishes between bodily desires and anger. Anger is said to follow reason and to be ultimately vanquished by reason when incontinently pursued.[22] Thus, anger is of a higher status than corporeal desire because anger is nearer to reason and more subject to its guidance. The discussion of anger implies a three-part distinction among reason, certain habits (including anger) which are cultivated by laws, and corporeal desires that are connected to the body. Aristotle calls the set of behaviors and attitudes cultivated through habitual obedience to the law more natural than the bodily desires. This seems clearly false, unless Aristotle is redefining *natural* to mean those things uniquely human. Habits are uniquely human insofar as they are the basis of moral virtue and responsibility; corporeal passions, however, are shared with the animal kingdom.

Habits like anger (or *thymos*) are uniquely human in that they allow citizens to pick and choose among the baser desires. In so doing, habits allow citizens to rise above corporeal desire and gain a measure of control or moral responsibility. Anger serves as the intermediary between reason and simple desire, and it takes its direction from that reason which speaks through the laws. In turn, anger tames the insolence of the desires and allows choice. But by allowing choice, anger becomes inextricably tied to any discussion of morals and moral responsibility. It is anger that supports continence, the ability to act on the knowledge of what is right despite the impertinent clamor of sensuous desire.

Ultimately, Aristotle's argument that moral virtue and politics can be reconciled rests on understanding politics in light of friendship, especially a friendship among good men. And this friendship depends not only on the knowledge of right conduct but also on the ability to act based on that knowledge—that is to say, on continence. Continence, however, depends on the proper cultivation of anger or *thymos* through habituation to obeying good laws. For anger supports the pride or self-regarding aspect of the magnanimous and just friend who would be ashamed to act immorally; anger supports the choice to deny the impulse to base pleasures. In this, anger is the ally of reason in supporting moral responsibility.

III. Kant and Aristotle: Implications for Retributive Justice

This essay began with the observation that some retributivists, such as Robinson, disagree with other retributivists, such as Berns, primarily over the following question: To which should the law and criminal justice system respond, the anger that citizens feel when they behold injustice or the dictates of formal, syllogistic reason which derive from categorical imperatives a logical structure of requirements establishing guilt or desert? The answer to that question turns ultimately on one's vision of human communities. For Professor Robinson, political life and civic communities originate with the acceptance as literally true of particular first principles or moral premises which are themselves philosophically disputable. Once debate is suspended on a particular set of moral first premises, political life emerges as rules of justice are formally deduced. One is tempted to accuse Professor Robinson of recommending complete rigidity on the definition of means (particularly political rights and responsibilities) to a wholly arbitrarily selected set of ends.

Curiously, Robinson never denies that citizens do feel angry when they experience injustice; he merely denies that the anger they experience is relevant to a discussion of justice or to the criminal justice system. As a practical matter, one should ask whether anger is better dealt with by excluding it from the criminal justice system altogether or by drawing it into the community's determination of justice, where it can be confronted with and modified by formal elements of constitutional procedure such as trial by jury and due process of law.

Excluding anger from moral discourse and repressing its voice in community life is dangerous. Aristotle himself pointed out that anger (when it escapes reason's direction) subverts rather than promotes choice and moral responsibility. By drawing anger into the criminal justice system, by allowing it at least equal legitimacy with compassion, anger can be tempered or guided. Denied a legitimate forum in the life of a community, anger will find a way to express itself; such expression, unguided by procedural and constitutional safeguards, leads all too easily to vigilantism and lynch law. To bring anger into a legitimate place in moral discourse is not to give it free rein; rather, it is to lend it guidance and, therefore, dignity.

The most penetrating criticism of Kantian ethics is offered by Aristotle's vision of human communities. Aristotle offers friendship as the benchmark by which justice and virtue should be understood. The very notion of friendship involves precisely those affective or emotive reactions, such as love, warmth, and fellow-feeling, that Robinson and Kant are so loath to admit to moral discussions. Indeed, Aristotle's presentation includes both friendship, which draws citizens through its pleasantness to be virtuous, and anger, which when guided by reason suppresses the baser desires and allows human life in its fullest and most natural sense to emerge.

Is it not the case that virtually all human beings engage in and take seriously discussions of justice? All around us in our daily lives, we hear citizens argue about what is just in their relations among one another. But those discussions are not formal, abstract, and logically deductive. Rather, they take place in highly particular human contexts which inevitably influence (but not determine) the debate. Kant would have us deny those contexts, or at least exclude them from a significant role in moral discourse. Aristotle gives such contexts a prominent role in his moral philosophy. Robinson and Kant offer a Socratic community apparently populated by wholly reasonable citizens—but is that a political community? Is that the type of community fit for citizens who care about one another, who seek to see one another dealt with justly?

In thinking about such political communities, Aristotle argued that the central focus must be on friendship, the community in light of which politics at its very best is understood. If this is so, then Professor Berns's argument is slightly, but significantly, out of focus. The fact that anger is necessary for morality to work does not mean that reliance on and encouragement of anger is in every case the right approach to law and morality. While Aristotle held that anger, continence, friendship, and morality were all bound up together, he explicitly argued that it was friendship by which politics, and therefore morality, ought to orient itself.

An examination of friendship as the most perfect of communities led Aristotle ultimately to consider anger as necessary to sustain morality. It is extremely doubtful whether an examination that begins with anger would necessarily lead to a recognition of friendship as the most perfect of communities. While anger is necessary for morality, it is friendship that is sufficient for morality. This order of priorities ought not to be obscured.

In conclusion, acknowledging that anger is relevant to criminal justice is part of a larger recognition that human life as we live it together in communities involves friendship and anger, love and resentment. And for this reason, a retributive theory grounded in a moral philosophy such as Aristotle's is more deserving of our consideration than the formal, abstract alternative offered by Robinson and Kant.

Notes

1. Karl Menninger, *The Crime of Punishment* (New York: Viking Press, 1968), p. 113.

2. Perhaps the most widely cited of the books advocating rehabilitation is Menninger's *Crime of Punishment*. An excellent statement of the social interventionist position is Ramsey Clark, *Crime in America* (New York: Simon & Schuster, 1970).

3. James Q. Wilson, *Thinking about Crime* (New York: Basic Books, 1975). See especially chapter 3.

4. Walter Berns, "Retribution as the Ground for Punishment," pp. 1–14 above.
5. Immanuel Kant, *Foundations of the Metaphysics of Morals,* trans. Lewis White Beck (Indianapolis: Bobbs-Merrill, 1959).
6. Ibid., p. 9.
7. Aristotle, *The Rhetoric, Poetic, and Nicomachean Ethics of Aristotle,* trans. Thomas Taylor (London: James Black and Sons, 1818), 2:52. (bk. 2, chap. 2).
8. Kant, *Foundations,* pp. 16–17.
9. Ibid., p. 29.
10. Ibid., p. 30.
11. Ibid., p. 44.
12. Ibid., p. 46.
13. Ibid., p. 47.
14. Immanuel Kant, "Idea for a Universal History from a Cosmopolitan Point of View," in *On History,* trans. Lewis White Beck et al. (Indianapolis: Bobbs-Merrill, 1963), p. 11.
15. Ibid., p. 16.
16. Ibid., p. 15.
17. Aristotle, *Ethics,* p. 409 (bk. 10, chap. 9).
18. Ibid., p. 25 (bk. 1, chap. 7).
19. Ibid., p. 59 (bk. 2, chap. 5).
20. Ibid., p. 62 (bk. 2, chap. 6).
21. Ibid., pp. 130, 155 (bk. 4, chap. 3; bk. 5, chap. 1).
22. Ibid., p. 261 (bk. 7, chap. 4).

Punishment and the Criminal Justice System: A Prosecutor's Viewpoint

WILLIAM J. KUNKLE, JR.

A well-respected criminal court judge made the following observation about the criminal justice system: It's the only game in the world where all the rules are in writing (and so detailed that they fill whole libraries), where the referee has robes instead of a striped shirt and can fine the players or lock them in jail for any violation of the rules, and yet only one side has to follow them. There is truth in this analysis as to both the system's concerns with "fairness" and the analogy to a game or game playing as now dignified by the social sciences. Another common observation of the criminal courts is that most successful prosecutors are frustrated "jocks" who have found a new arena in which to compete.

These may be oversimplifications, but they give some insight to the prosecutor's view of punishment. The overriding factor is, to use Norval Morris's terminology, the *appropriateness* of the punishment. Such a perspective encompasses (or may be a part of) the retributive theory of punishment but is also connected with the theory of postconviction preventive detention. Before discussing how prosecutors apply appropriateness of punishment in actual practice, it is necessary to examine some of these factors which give the retributive theory preeminence for us and which tend to minimize or eliminate other theories of punishment, such as deterrence or rehabilitation.

I. The Education of a Prosecutor

Most law school graduates, even those applying for positions with prosecutor's offices, leave law school with a distinctly liberal viewpoint (when compared to society at large) and with an affinity for the defense in criminal cases. I make this assertion based on the review of résumés, legal writing samples, and personal interviews of 80 to 120 final contenders for employment as assistant state's attorneys of Cook County for each of the past five years.

This observation is supported by the direction and content of the law school experience with respect to the criminal law. Many, if not most, professors of criminal law are or have been defense lawyers. Constitutional law classes focus on the United States Supreme Court's expansion of the individual's (criminal defendant's) rights against the state (the People). Legal clinic experience is a holy crusade on behalf of "indigent" defendants. Advanced study projects or special research assignments deal with federal appeals of capital defendants whose convictions have been affirmed several times before the eager law student gets a chance to blow "Gideon's Trumpet." Seminars on "Law and Society" feature *Soul on Ice* by Eldridge Cleaver, *The Crime of Punishment* by Karl Menninger, guest lectures by '60s "cause" lawyers, and authors like Tom Wicker and Norman Mailer.

Notwithstanding the liberal influence of the law schools, most experienced felony trial prosecutors are decidedly conservative with respect to criminal justice issues. I would suggest that this metamorphosis arises from three learned realizations. First, they learn that there is indeed a broad range of crimes and offenses in the system—from the neighborhood squabbles, the juvenile "status" crimes, and the gambling violations at the corner tavern to the often almost unbelievably cruel and vicious violent offenses (Charles E. Silberman refers to "garbage cases" versus "real crimes").[1] But of more importance to the issue at hand, they learn that the quantity of real crimes is enormous and their quality truly horrendous.

Second, these prosecutors learn that the vast majority of real crimes are committed by repeat offenders. The usually quoted recidivism rate of 33 percent (that is, one in three convicted offenders returns to crime), is very misleading.[2] In the felony courts in Cook County, for example, defendants' criminal histories are evaluated by the number of pages, not the number of entries. More often than not, the only one-page "rap sheets" belong to defendants under twenty-one years of age, since arrests and convictions before age seventeen do not appear on State Bureau of Identification records.

James Q. Wilson has pointed out several ways of looking at recidivism. He notes that over 87 percent of those arrested will have been previously arrested, or the probability of rearrest is .87, very nearly a certainty.[3] He also cited the research of Marvin Wolfgang on ten thousand Philadelphia boys born in 1945 which concluded that once a juvenile had been arrested three times, his chances of being rearrested were over 70 percent.

Without reference to research studies, prosecutors are well aware of the tremendous rate of recidivism with respect to particular crimes and particular criminals. Narcotics addicts have numerous arrests not only for drug charges but also usually for burglary, theft, shoplifting, prostitution, and sometimes armed robbery. Whether or not all or most rapes and other sex crimes are "caused" by mental problems, the offenders who commit them are repeaters. Burglars and armed robbers, whether skillful or not, often practice their crimes as a trade or profession over a long period of time. Murder is often regarded as a non-recidivist offense (leading to the red-herring deterrence argument over the death penalty); in fact, all too many murderers have been tried or convicted of murder before, and still larger numbers have prior arrests or convictions for weapons violations, aggravated batteries, and attempted murders.

Third, they learn that even though the system can and must arrive at a determination as to what the facts are, what the defendant's status is, and what an appropriate sentence is, this determination is subject to radical change, over a very long period of time, without regard to the correctness or justice of the determination itself. They learn that they must fight a long, hard battle to get the system to "do the right thing,"[4] and then fight a longer and harder battle to keep the correct decision intact.

II. Rehabilitation

No experienced prosecutor is opposed to rehabilitation. But it occurs so infrequently with serious adult criminals that neither the criminal justice system nor the correctional system should be designed to rely upon it. In *Deathwork,* a long-suffering correctional supervisor at a mythical Florida prison responds to the cry for rehabilitation on the eve of five executions of murderers: " 'The word rehabilitation,' he would drawl in a hard-boiled monotone he reserved for the quote, 'presupposes habilitation. But the people who come to prison are not habilitated in the first place. Therefore there is no such thing as rehabilitation, because you can't rehabilitate a nonhabilitated man.' "[5]

Henry Brisbon was seventeen years old when he committed the "I-57" murders. Henry and his armed-robber friends rear-ended unsuspecting motorists on an Illinois expressway. When the victims pulled over to assess the damage and discuss insurance with Brisbon, he would rob them at shotgun point, lead them off into the weeds, and kill them. He said he told an engaged couple to "kiss their last kiss" before he blew them out of their shoes. On another occasion, he forced his young victim to strip naked and plead for her life. He then shoved his shotgun barrel into her vagina and fired. As he described it to his cousin, while jingling the keys and change in his pocket for effect, "she twitched and flopped around for five minutes like a big white snake." He then shot her in the neck, ending his sport for the night. Because he was not yet eighteen when he committed these murders, Brisbon was not eligible for the death penalty under Illinois law. He was sentenced to life without parole. While incarcerated in Stateville, he stabbed a trustee to death with a homemade "shank." Now over eighteen, he was sentenced to death in Will County after being convicted of his fourth murder. Housed on death row in Menard Correctional Center in Chester, Illinois, he recently attempted to kill another inmate, stabbing him five times with a cell-made weapon. While retreating from that assault, he also stabbed mass murderer John Gacy in the arm with the same weapon.

Notwithstanding a diminished sympathy for John Gacy and perhaps other death-row inmates, the right of even these individuals to the safety of their persons as well as that of the other prisoners, the guards, and the civilian employees shows the necessity of the death penalty and the insufficiency of the life sentence. Likewise, Henry Brisbon, Steven Judy, and the thousands of other violent offenders who have never been "habilitated" demonstrate the futility of reliance on rehabilitation.

If our society can develop truly successful methods of rehabilitation, they should be employed primarily in habilitating—in the schools, the communities, the churches, and the families. Their *secondary* use should be in the juvenile and family court setting and in the first offender and misdemeanor offense context. Only when such precious resources are adequately available for these tasks should efforts be made to provide them for that small percentage of real criminals who may be willing to allow themselves to be rehabilitated.

III. Deterrence

Plato wrote that a criminal must be punished "in order that, in the future times, he and those who see him corrected, may utterly hate injustice, or at any rate abate much of their evil-doing."[6] The basic concept of the deterrent effect of punishment makes sense now as it did then. That it actually works is known to every parent, drill sergeant, and police officer.

Dr. Karl Menninger says that "the swift, on-the-spot infliction of sufficiently painful stimulation to sufficiently influence animals—dogs or human beings—will tend to dissuade them from certain types of behavior of which we do not approve and which we wish to teach them not to do. But it does not deter others not so treated. . . . It is facile and fallacious to assume from this fact that human beings in general can be conditioned by threats of punishment or by the delayed infliction of penalties of attenuated painfulness from yielding to the temptation of impulsive crimes." Dr. Menninger goes on to point out that "drunken driving is almost nonexistent in Scandinavia, where the sureness, swiftness, and severity of the penalty is well known."[7] His criticisms of unduly delayed or unfairly administered punishments may be well taken, but this does not justify the obvious contradiction between his statements. It is plain that all Scandinavians have not been personally punished for drunken driving. Therefore, such punishment of others must in fact deter those not so punished. As to the delay and fairness issues, the proper course is to address attention and resources to the solution of these problems where and if they exist. (The issue of "undue delay" will be discussed briefly later with reference to preventive detention.) Rejecting punishment generally or punishment for deterrence specifically because of these problems would be a classic "bathwater and baby" solution.

Statistical attacks on the deterrent value of punishment usually deal with the death penalty. For the most part, they reach their conclusions on the basis of questionable data and even more suspect premises. As Walter Berns concludes: "Hanging is not a deterrent, we are told with some frequency; but such statements derive from partisan commitment, not science."[8]

The first-hand view confirms the reality of deterrence. Until recently, Chicago (the Municipal Division of the Circuit Court of Cook County) had a group of specially assigned courts known as "boys' courts." These courts handled most of the felony preliminary hearings for male offenders between the ages of seventeen and twenty-one. (Murders, sex crimes, auto thefts and narcotics cases were handled in other specialized courts.) The antique rationale was that these youthful offenders should be handled differently, or at least separately, from the older, "hardened" criminals and necessarily (by statute) not in juvenile court.

In 1976, the last full year of the boys' courts existence, the following percentages of some index crimes were committed by offenders from age eighteen to age twenty:

Murder	20.9%
Rape	23.1%
Aggravated assault	13.2%
Robbery	21.4%

It should also be noted that offenders under eighteen committed an even larger percentage of serious offenses (39 percent for all index crimes against 17.5 percent for all index crimes for the 18–20-year age group). Each group was responsible for a much greater percentage of serious crime than their numbers relative to the entire population would suggest. (Adding these groups together gives a total of 56.5 percent of index crimes for offenders twenty years old and younger; the total of those twenty-four years old and younger was 72.3 percent.)

Despite the fact that these "youth" were a greater actual threat to the community than their "hardened" elders, the system held on to the myth of the boys' court until 1977. These courts were set up geographically, and their cases came from one or two of the Chicago Police Department's six areas. Because of this geographic system, district and tactical officers and area investigators knew not only the youthful serious repeat offenders in their area but also the judge regularly sitting in their area's boys' court. The differences between "stiff" and "soft" judges could be felt on the street and would eventually be reflected by the size of the court calls for that particular branch. Whenever a "stiff" judge controlled the action, the size of the court call would gradually shrink. During one six-month reign of a tough and streetwise judge, the call was reduced by fully one-half. When such a jurist was replaced by a "softball," the number of cases and the problems on the street grew quite rapidly. There was no doubt in the officers' minds that punishments given affected the attitude of these youthful offenders. Officers often were told, "Why bother to pick me up for a crummy burglary? Judge So and So's going to turn me loose or give me probation again anyway."

Those of us who deal with serious violent offenders all the time know that punishment is a valid deterrent. When capital punishment was not enforced in Illinois and when '60s judges and juries were working in an overburdened system, lots of burglars made a conscious decision to carry guns. Lots of rapists and armed robbers decided that killing victims and witnesses was the cost-effective way to do business. Lots of street soldiers and gang-narcotics-enforcers decided that the rewards of their profession were worth a remotely possible eight to eleven years they would probably have to serve on a murder conviction.

Lately in Cook County, because of legislative changes, prosecutorial stiffening, expansion of the system, and subtle but definite attitudinal changes among judges and juries, the message is reaching the streets. And the index crime rate has been steadily decreasing or holding its own against lowering economic conditions. It may be true that some types of murders (domestic quarrels, for example) may not be deterred through effective punishment, and that there may be a very large pool of potential narcotics dealers, but I believe that neither of these factors applies to other criminals such as robbers, and especially armed robbers.

I have always optimistically believed that there is a finite number of citizens in any given community who, for whatever reasons, are willing to put a gun in someone's face and say "your money or your life." Therefore, I have concluded that longer sentences and surer convictions for these people will in fact deter them, and others like them, to a degree that should be noticeable. In 1972 there were 23,531 robberies in Chicago, or 705.7 per 100,000 population. In 1976 there were 17,577 robberies, or 571.8 per 100,000 population. In 1979 there were 14,464 robberies, or 487.1 per 100,000 population.[9] In contrast to these decreases, both suburban and rural counties other than Cook showed marked raw and percentage increases, and suburban Cook County remained fairly constant with some decreases.[10] (Comparisons were based on robbery convictions rather than arrests.)

Conversely, the area in which our system is failing to utilize an available deterrent factor is the realm of the "upper-class" drug dealer. One Cook County judge is reputed to have stated that no citizen of this country should go to the penitentiary for using or selling drugs. The State's Attorney's Office of Cook County has sought writs of mandamus for several judges who have sentenced drug offenders to less than the statutory minimums for possession or sale of cocaine, in particular. In one extreme case, a judge who refused to send two white, young, middle-class sisters to the penitentiary after finding them guilty of the possession and delivery of more than the amount requiring a class X penalty (six-year minimum) was ordered to issue such a sentence by the Illinois Supreme Court. The burgeoning crop of students, businesspersons, and professionals who are dabbling and specializing in the lucrative field of marijuana, cocaine, or pill trafficking is ripe for the deterrent effect of sure and severe sentences. So long as they think that they can't do worse than probation, the tremendous profits will outweigh the somewhat minimal risks. These people are aware of what both the market prices and the "market sentences" are at any given time and in any given place. The word will reach them, and many of them will heed it.

IV. Preventive Detention

The criminal justice system actually uses two forms of preventive detention: pretrial and posttrial. Pretrial preventive detention (incarceration as opposed to release on bail or recognizance) is constitutionally (federal or state) limited to persons charged with capital offenses or other narrow categories of persons charged with committing felonies while on bail or parole for other felony convictions.[11] Most state constitutions and many court decisions interpreting the federal constitutional right to bail prohibit a broader application of pretrial detention for purposes of public protection. The only purpose of bail considered valid is to insure appearance in court, with the limitations expressed above.

The final report of the Attorney General's Task Force on Violent Crime included recommendation 38:

> The Attorney General should support or propose legislation to amend the Bail Reform Act that would accomplish the following:
>
> a. Permit courts to deny bail to persons who are found by clear and

convincing evidence to present a danger to particular persons or the community.

b. Deny bail to a person accused of a serious crime who had previously, while in pretrial release status, committed a serious crime for which he was convicted.

c. Codify existing case law defining the authority of the courts to detain defendants as to whom no conditions of release are adequate to assure appearance at trial.

d. Abandon, in the case of serious crimes, the current standard presumptively favoring release of convicted persons awaiting imposition or execution of sentence or appealing their convictions.

e. Provide the government with the right to appeal release decisions analogous to the appellate rights now afforded to defendants.

f. Require defendants to refrain from criminal activity as a mandatory condition of release.

g. Make the penalties for bail jumping more closely proportionate to the penalties for the offense with which the defendant was originally charged.[12]

If the Congress was to enact any or all of these changes, they would immediately affect only those charged with federal offenses. However, once tested for constitutionality, similar laws would be available to the states, and many would doubtless enact them.

Prosecutors, well familiar with the staggering number of serious offenses committed by violent offenders while on bail, are very much in favor of such appropriately limited uses of pretrial detention. In Illinois, all felony defendants incarcerated while awaiting trial must be tried within 120 days of arrest or be released, unless they request a delay.[13] Thus, the local news teams' heartrending story about the poor murderer waiting five years to be tried must be taken with a very large grain of salt. Defendants who wait more than 120 days (while in jail) for their trials do so because they and their attorneys well know that criminal cases do not improve with age.

It is just such "undue" pretrial delays, coupled with jail and court system overcrowding, that opponents of pretrial preventive detention point to in their defense of every defendant's unalienable right to release on bail. In Cook County (except for the reality of occasional jail overcrowding), the facts do not support such arguments. At the end of 1981, only 794 of the 6,299 felony cases pending had been initiated in prior years.[14] In other words, only 12.6 percent of the cases were over one year old, including not just incarcerated defendants but all defendants awaiting trial. On August 16, 1979, the Chicago Crime Commission released a study on delay in the felony trial courts of the Circuit Court of Cook County. Based on random sampling of dispositions in five courtrooms over a three-month period, they concluded that the average time from arrest to trial was fifteen months. Since that time, information on the time from arrest to trial has been recorded with respect to every felony disposition by the State's Attorney's Office. For all felony dispositions during 1981, the average time from arrest to trial was 6.3 months (this figure includes the Felony Trial Division—11,680 dispositions; the First District (Chicago) Preliminary Hearing Courts—3,721 dispositions; and the Suburban Districts' Preliminary Hearing Courts—750 dispositions). If only the Felony Trial Division is included (as with the 1979 Crime Commission Report), the average for 1981 was 8.4 months from arrest to trial.

Further, the simple truth is that even though aware of the utility of delay as a defense tactic, defendants in custody usually are less willing to request delays than are those on bond. At least in Cook County, judicial and prosecutorial resources are available to afford a speedy trial to any defendant who either wants one or is willing to have one. These improvements in delay have been achieved in spite of a consistent overall conviction rate (about 90 percent) and an ever-increasing percentage of dispositions by trial (less and less plea bargaining).[15] Limited pretrial preventive detention thus could be employed here without serious consequences to "the system."

Posttrial preventive detention is institutionalization for the purpose of protecting the public from the offender. For prosecutors, it is probably the most important and most valuable tool in their effort to perform their duty to protect the public. The obvious benefit to society is that the individual offender is prevented from victimizing innocent citizens, at least for the time he or she is locked up. Considering the rates of recidivism and the allegedly poor rates of crime solution, this is no small benefit to society in and of itself.

If recent theories about a "burnout point" for violent criminals are correct, then serious or repeat offenders should, for the protection of society, be incarcerated for mandatory periods which would insure their release after this point. The creation of career criminal courts and life sentences for three violent felony convictions are steps in this direction in Illinois and other states.

Grudgingly recognizing a rehabilitation-oriented correctional system's lack of success with serious criminals, Illinois and several other states have scrapped the indeterminate sentence-parole release system in favor of flat-time sentencing and the abolition of classical parole. This "new" theory of sentencing was generated by David Fogel, then the executive director of the Illinois Law Enforcement Commission. Flat-time sentencing was designed to give tighter limits on judicial discretion (to improve consistency of sentencing), to give certainty to the defendant's expected term (to improve control in institutions), to eliminate the parole board's deciding upon release (again to improve certainty and to remove insincere participation in rehabilitation activities for the sole purpose of conning the board), and to eliminate the costly and ineffective parole supervision system. This initial planning evolved into Governor James Thompson's much-publicized class X crime legislation, marketed as a "get tough" package. In many respects it was. However, the sentencing ranges finally enacted (like Fogel's slightly different originals) were carefully chosen to decrease, not increase, the overall burden on the state correctional system. When the new day-for-a-day good time credits are applied to either set of sentencing averages, the average projected prison stay for all crimes except murder and armed robbery is reduced. Expected terms for murder are slightly increased, and for armed robbery less so.[16]

Prosecutors can understand, but not necessarily forgive, the correctional system's consistent battle to prevent actual longer sentences. Mandatory day-for-a-day good time is merely a sham. Neither individual victims nor the public in general expects a ten-year sentence to mean five years. Even more distressing to citizens and prosecutors is the recent abuse of "good conduct credit" for awards of up to 270 days of sentence credit for no purpose other than reducing prison population.[17] Certain federal court decisions and pending cases have exacerbated this problem.

The negligible benefits of the old parole system that accompanied indeterminate sentences will not be missed, the certainty of flat time should help in several areas, and the realization that every violent criminal cannot be rehabilitated is a step forward. But the failure to provide both the physical resources and the legislative support for sentences consistent with the public's right to the protection of its government is inexcusable.

V. Retribution

Prosecutors have a tremendous amount of discretion with respect to what happens in any individual felony case. Whether to charge, what to charge, what special penalties to seek, and what sentence to recommend after trial or to accept in a plea conference are all properly within their authority.

Much of a prosecutor's most important training through experience is learning "what a case is worth." Evaluating cases correctly and fairly is the essence of good prosecutors. They learn these lessons from widely separated points of view. They must deal with the anguish of the victims and their families; they come to prosecutors for revenge, often with impossible expectations. They cannot understand why the judge should be polite or patient with defense attorneys, much less defendants. They cannot accept a plea of guilty, even to an appropriate sentence, because they have been denied their day in court. They cannot, and perhaps should not, accept the legal hypocrisies of the exclusionary rule or the insanity defense.

Prosecutors must work with the police. Despite their superior knowledge of and limited acceptance of the rules and routines of the legal system, their viewpoint is not that different from the victim's. Veteran investigators will not hesitate to overpower the green prosecutor with their knowledge of the street and the system, to try to achieve their personal view of the correct outcome.

Prosecutors represent "The People of Illinois," but many judges think they work for them. A judge can use many tools to mold a prosecutor. The name of the game for most judges is dispositions. Not long jury trials, not careful motion hearings, not exhaustive considerations of sentencing alternatives, but rather, "how many cases can we get rid of today?" Contrary to the spirit (if not the letter) of Illinois law, a judge who disagrees with the prosecutor's refusal to reduce an armed robbery charge (class X, six-year minimum) to a robbery charge (probationable) can simply tell the defense attorney to "take a bench trial and I'll find him guilty of robbery and give him probation." The state cannot appeal a finding of not guilty.

Prosecutors must deal with the press. They or their superiors may have to run for reelection. Their careful research and brilliant argument on an important point of law will not reach print, but the "human interest" aspect of the dope dealer-murderer's "honor student" background may well be on page 1.

Finally, prosecutors must deal with an entire establishment of organized defense lawyers, public defenders, probation officers, social workers, psychiatrists, and pressure groups which exist solely to protect the rights of the defendant.

After dealing with all of these factions day after day, in hundreds of cases, they must decide what a case is worth—what a just, appropriate, right, correct sentence is for the facts of this case and the background of this defendant. There may be more than one answer. What is right and what is practicable or possible are not always the same. In any event, having evaluated all of the aforementioned factors and others, prosecutors decide what the appropriate sentence should be. This sentence, if truly appropriate, will adequately serve as retribution. It must satisfy the reasonable expectation of revenge of the victim, the victim's family, and the victim's society. If it achieves this result it will also protect the public from this offender, deter others to the degree that it is publicized and promptly executed, and provide society with the measure of fairness necessary to replace the vendetta with the court.

Those who fault retributive sentencing for lacking integrity argue that there should be a uniformity of just deserts that will satisfy some perfect scheme of proportionality (presumably as defined by the critic) and at the same time survive the most intricate statistical scrutiny into its invariance or uniform application. One response to these arguments has been the grid system advanced in Minnesota. A system of factors supposedly quantifying the defendant's background in both positive and negative terms is cross-graphed with factors quantifying the seriousness of the offense committed. The major problem with such a system is, as usual, who gets to assign the quantum values? As with the "get tough" Class X mandatory sentencing structure in Illinois, it is the State Department of Corrections (amazingly in concert with the civil libertarian factions) that ensures that no matter what factors and what values are opted for, the net result is a lower penitentiary population.

The answer to proportionality and invariance is not a simple chart or a set of mathematical equations. Rather, it is the complex process of the public expression of appropriateness through elected representatives in the legislature and in the trial and appellate courts. One need only look to the new mandatory minimum sentence for residential burglary to see the downstate or rural Illinois citizens' evaluation of and response to the treatment of burglars. A comprehensive revision of Illinois's definition and treatment of sexual offenses is the direct result of pressure on the legislature from women's groups, largely Chicago based. For good or ill, these are clear examples of the People (or the citizens, or the public, or the victims) deciding what is appropriate.

Once these expressions have been made law, they are refined by trial and appellate judges (also elected by the People) who have many powers to modify, amplify, or negate the intent of the legislative changes. The Chicago judge who reduces a residential burglary to "regular" burglary for a sentence of probation on a plea of guilty is not likely to be criticized in the Chicago *Tribune* when the complainant cannot be located and is not present in court for the sentencing. However, the small-town downstate judge who must attend the Lions Club meetings with the victim and his neighbors, and who knows the content of his sentencing remarks will be on page 1 of the local paper, no doubt will send the defendant to the penitentiary for a minimum of four years.

Integrity critics will herein find manifest variance and a failing of just deserts. If grids and arithmetic are to decide the issue, they are right. But are these results unacceptably inappropriate? Just as communities' attitudes toward a residential burglary may differ, doesn't the offender's attitude or awareness of the potential penalty vary with the community? Can it be appropriate (moral) for two different jurisdictions to have a different notion of what a particular crime or case is "worth" in punishment?

The Fifth Circuit Court of Appeals has ruled that just such a difference between communities within a state is not only appropriate but constitutional. The Louisiana death penalty laws provide for a proportionality review of all death sentences.[18] This review is conducted not on the basis of a statewide comparison but rather on a comparison of first-degree murder cases from the particular judicial district (parish) in which the sentence on review was issued. I would conclude that if judicial review of the appropriateness of death sentences in terms of just deserts and invariance can be on a district-by-district basis, then a variance in the "price" of a burglary from one region of a state to another should not result in constitutional problems, much less moral ones.

In addition to the existing system's ability to arrive at pragmatically appropriate sentences for the vast array of crimes and criminals, an operative system of proportionality review exists for all sentences. That system is the state appellate court system and the separate system of federal district and appellate court review. With reviewing courts providing the leveling influence of proportionality review and legislatures narrowing the breadth of judicial discretion in sentencing, the evils of undeserved or variant sentences simply don't exist in the real world to a degree sufficient to overcome the benefits of retributive sentencing.

VI. Inappropriate Outcome in the Guise of Fairness

Two sacred cows of the criminal and constitutional law that lead to inappropriate outcomes (inappropriate punishment or absence of punishment) are the exclusionary rule and the insanity defense. These anomalies are not central to the issues here but are connected sufficiently to warrant brief discussion.

The Exclusionary Rule

The exclusionary rule, entirely manufactured by United States Supreme Court decision, provides for the exclusion of evidence from a criminal trial where such evidence has been obtained in violation of the defendant's constitutional rights (the right to freedom from unreasonable search and seizure, for example). In theory, it punishes law enforcement officers for the purpose of encouraging them to respect the citizen's rights.

In fact, police are not punished at all (prosecutors and society are), and criminals are rewarded. Most police officers who make unwarranted traffic stops in high crime areas, based on "mere suspicion," and then conduct unreasonably broad searches of vehicles to find drugs, alcohol, or firearms, are doing so primarily to get the guns or drugs off the street. Some would argue the primary motive is less salutary—to oppress or roust economic or ethnic groups, or to get credit for another arrest. None of these motives is directed toward a conviction; the arrest and seizure are the ends in themselves. Only frustrated prosecutors and the public are punished: prosecutors lose their cases and must explain their poor statistics, while the public must pay for the courts, judges, jails, clerks, and so on to do nothing but dismiss hundreds of gun and narcotics cases every day because of "a bad stop." The public pays an even bigger price when these nickel-and-dime rulings suddenly are applied to the Richard Speck or John Gacy cases and not tax dollars but public safety is sacrificed.

The most bitter irony of the exclusionary rule is that it creates this system of redress for police violation of constitutional rights only for those who break the law. An innocent citizen whose home is unlawfully searched and damaged by narcotics agents who find no drugs cannot move to suppress the evidence because there is no prosecution and no evidence. The innocent citizen is given only the remedies of civil suits for damages, police board or other administrative forms of review of officers' actions, and federal civil rights suits. Neither the legislatures nor the United States Supreme Court has been constrained to create additional remedies for the innocent citizen. (And hundreds and thousands of searches with or without warrants fail to turn up contraband month after month, year after year.)

Why, then, should a person unlawfully possessing drugs, guns, gambling paraphernalia, or a murder weapon have a system of legal remedies not available to an innocent citizen suffering exactly the same intrusion? Why especially when such a system results in injustice and inappropriate punishment?

If a principled society must retain integrity of its criminal justice system, its acts (the acts of its law enforcers) must conform not to the philosopher's or theologian's moral proscriptions but rather to that society's even body of law. The fact is that police officers adhere to those proscriptions far more than the ACLU and the defense bar would lead the public to believe. To rail against appropriate punishment because of imagined or real violations of the Fourth Amendment is another "baby and bathwater" position.

With or without a "good-faith exception," the exclusionary rule will remain as the primary means of enforcing the Fourth Amendment and protecting the "integrity" of law enforcement.[19] What is needed in addition is not the repudiation of appropriate punishment but rather swiftly applied civil remedies for the injured citizen (innocent or not) and legal and administrative punishment for offending officers.

The Insanity Defense

Other writers for this volume have beautifully and correctly stated the philosophical and moral-legal absurdity of the insanity defense, and I shall not attempt to redo what they have done. Advocates of the insanity defense, as currently used in the United States, often point to the fact that it is used in less than 1 percent of the felony cases and is the cornerstone of a just legal system. As a practical matter, even assuming that both arguments are correct, this area is still deserving of attention and reform.

Even if the insanity defense is used rarely, it is used most often in homicides, where proof of factual guilt is great, and usually in cases with great media and public interest. Therefore, the end result of inappropriate punishment (often none) is widely publicized, and the general public holds the law in disrepute. The people of this country saw John Hinckley shoot the president of the United States. They know Hinckley planned it in advance, purchased weapons and ammunition, stalked his target, lay in ambush, aimed, and consciously pulled the trigger more than once. The public's definition of criminal intent and criminal responsibility includes the actions of John Hinckley; the law's definition, at least according to one jury, does not. Therein lies the rub.

Either the legal definition of insanity is wrong; or the judge's instructions on that definition were wrong; or the rules of evidence permitting experts to testify about motivation rather than criminal intent, and on the basis of analytical theory rather than scientific fact, were wrong; or the people's common sense is wrong (perhaps some or all of the above). In any case, there is a clear difference between the citizen's view and that jury's view as molded by the legal system.

More telling than this isolated example is the clear difference between the decisions of judges versus juries in insanity cases. Over the past ten years in Cook County there have been roughly 400 verdicts or findings of not guilty by reason of insanity. Of these, 4 were jury verdicts and about 396 were the decisions of judges hearing bench trials. Like the wise courtiers of the fable, the learned judges are apparently able to see the emperor's new clothes. The ordinary citizens, despite the common sense that lawyers and judges always tell them to rely on, alas, cannot.

Psychiatry and psychology are not yet sciences, and expert testimony in these fields in criminal cases is not entitled to the free reign given to traditional scientific testimony. Neither the experts, nor the lawyers, nor the judges can all agree on what the definitions are and what they mean. More specific yet simpler language is needed in instructions, definitions, and verdict forms.

These modest proposals are possible now partly because of the media and public reaction to the Hinckley verdict. Perhaps the preferable solution of abolishing the defense entirely and returning to the correct issue—was there criminal intent?—can ultimately be achieved. Either course will lead to more appropriate results.

VII. Conclusion

The prosecutor's view, or more correctly my view, of punishment incorrectly may be judged as harsh by some, lacking in compassion by many, and expensive in tax dollars for prisons by most. It is founded on a basic feeling of and respect for fairness, for the rules of the game. "Reforms" offered by social scientists and defense attorneys masquerading as academicians should not be substituted for the citizens' and the prosecutors' shared, commonsense desire to see the guilty punished appropriately regardless of technical errors by law enforcement or protestations of "society's-at-fault" psychiatrists.

To truly be the champion of the people, we must occasionally take a swing at the referee, knowing that an appropriate penalty may be forthcoming. Al McGuire and Bobby Knight are not alone in the knowledge that the officiating is not likely to be evenhanded if only one side gripes about the bad calls.

Notes

1. Charles E. Silberman, *Criminal Violence, Criminal Justice* (New York: Random House, 1978), p. 311.
2. Ibid., p. 373; Daniel Glaser, *The Effectiveness of a Prison and Parole System* (Indianapolis: Bobbs-Merrill, 1969), chaps. 2 and 3.
3. James Q. Wilson, *Thinking about Crime* (New York: Vintage Books, 1977), p. 181
4. A favorite phrase of supervisors in prosecutors' offices who are pressed for very specific advice and instead pass the buck to the assistant.
5. James McLendon, *Deathwork* (Philadelphia and New York: J.B. Lippincott, 1977), p. 30.
6. *The Great Ideas: A Syntopican of Great Books of the Western World*, 2 (Chicago: Encyclopaedia Britannica, 1952): 448–95.
7. Karl Menninger, *The Crime of Punishment* (New York: Viking Press, 1969), pp. 208, 209.
8. Walter Berns, *For Capital Punishment* (New York: Basic Books, 1979), pp. 96–97.

9. Statistical Analysis Center, *Violent Crime in Illinois* (Springfield: State of Illinois, Law Enforcement Commission, March 1981), p. 32.

10. Ibid.; Illinois Department of Corrections, *Statistical Presentation 1980* (Springfield: State of Illinois, October 1981), pp. 13, 18.

11. Illinois Revised Statutes, 1981, chap. 38, arti. 110, secs. 4, 6.

12. *Attorney General's Task Force on Violent Crime: Final Report* (Washington, D.C.: U.S. Department of Justice, 0–353-069, August 17, 1981), p. 50.

13. Illinois Revised Statutes, 1981, chap. 38, arti. 103, sec. 5.

14. *1981 Annual Report to the Supreme Court of Illinois,* issued by the Administrative Office of the Illinois Courts.

15. Ibid.

16. David Fogel, *Testimony Prepared for the House Judiciary Committee II of the Illinois General Assembly* (Springfield: State of Illinois, September 11, 1975).

17. Illinois Revised Statutes, 1981, chap. 38, arti. 1003, sec. 6–3-(a)-(3).

18. The United States Supreme Court has held that proportionality review of death sentences is not required by the Constitution. See *Pulley* v. *Harris,* 79 L. Ed. 2d 29 (1984). However, where such a procedure is required by state law, it must be applied constitutionally.

19. See *U.S.* v. *Leon,* 44 CCH S. Ct. Bull., p. B4928, Docket no. 82–1771, decided 7/05/84, wherein the United States Supreme Court created a good-faith exception to the exclusionary rule.

The Integrity of the Retributive Ideal

JEROME H. SKOLNICK

Most philosophical analyses of punishment consider the traditional justifications for confining citizens in jails or prisons. These, of course, include deterrence, rehabilitation, incapacitation (sheer confinement for the purpose of keeping criminals off the streets), and retribution (desert as a portion of justice). The fashion in American jurisprudence has swung away from a concern with treating the criminal—can he or she be reshaped so that prospective criminality will be inhibited?—to the criminal's just deserts. Here the question has become: Did the criminal receive the punishment deserved for the acts committed?

A number of reasons can be adduced to account for the trend away from rehabilitation: disenchantment with the possibilities of reforming the offender, sentencing disparity under indeterminate sentencing structures, rising crime rates, and an even higher rise in the public's fear of crime. I am not going to undertake a sociological analysis of sentencing fashions. Instead, I plan to explore the principles underlying a retributive model—in order to clarify the conditions for the integrity of a justice system based on this model. I argue that, just as the rehabilitative ideal can be debased by converting treatment into custody and commitment into punishment,[1] so can the retributive ideal be debased by the methods used to collect evidence, by practicing "selective incapacitation" in sentencing, and by substandard conditions of imprisonment. By taking the reader on a walk through selected stages of the criminal justice system, I shall try to show that the aspiration to a principled retributive system is constantly challenged by consequentialist considerations; and that, paradoxically, we might reach the goal of principled retribution—not simply vengeance—by insisting upon less punishment rather than more.

Integrity

The idea of integrity has been discussed less by philosophers of law than by ethical philosophers, those concerned primarily with individual choice. Thus, Bernard Williams argues that integrity depends not on balancing consequences but on being true to one's own principles.[2] The greater good might require that we lie, steal, even kill; integrity might require that we do none of these.

Integrity might at first seem to be the equivalent of morality, but on reflection it is not. Moral ideals can and do vary across cultures. "A morality," writes Thomas Nagel, "with its ordering of virtues and prohibitions, provides a particular ideal of humanity in an ideal way of life."[3] Thus, morality can be relative, while integrity cannot. Integrity connotes fidelity to a particular ideal of humanity, while morality suggests the elaboration of the ideal. Thus, devout Roman Catholics and Jews can debate over the morality of food taboos. If, however, a self-proclaimed devout Jew ate pork with Christian friends to facilitate business dealings, he would be lacking in integrity. The Catholic, by contrast, would not be debasing his own ideal merely by eating pork, but would if he violated his Lenten promises in order to ingratiate himself with a business associate.

To have integrity, a criminal justice system must in a similar way remain true to its promises and principles. It is not even enough to observe, as in the ringing words of Justice Clark, that "Nothing can destroy a government more quickly than its failure to observe its own laws, or worse, its disregard of the charter of its own existence."[4] Actually, that may or may not be true. One can conceive of instances where a government might flourish by violating its own charter. The point is not survival; a government which violates its own charter cannot also claim to have acted with integrity—consistency with its own ideals.

A principled retributive system, possessing real integrity, must offer significant protections to those accused and convicted of crime. Thus, H. L. A. Hart's retributive model introduces integrity into punishment by limiting the punisher. Although Hart maintains that people should be punished for harms they have deliberately inflicted upon others, an accused may not be punished unless it is proved that he has actually done something wrong; and there must be a relationship between the offense and the severity of the punishment. The implications of Hart's conception need to be explored further by discussing the integrity of criminal justice.

If the substantive law embodies the morality of criminal justice, criminal procedure—the rule of law—seems to embody the criminal justice system's expression of integrity. As such, it imposes substantial restraints upon the way officials may go about enforcing the law, as well as on the way the law may be formulated. Hart, for example, in his prolegomenon to the principles of punishment, objects gravely "to those theories of law which in the interest of simplicity or uniformity obscure the distinction between primary laws setting standards for behavior and secondary laws specifying what officials must or may do when they are broken."[5] The idea of integrity of process suggests that there is an inextricable link between primary and secondary laws. It is one thing to insist that the guilty be punished; it is another to say that they must be punished properly. The latter represents the integrity of the retributive ideal.

Assuming we wish to punish properly, difficult issues arise when we ask what officials may or must do in determining that someone is justly deserving. Suppose a policeman has before him an individual whom he strongly believes on the basis of circumstantial evidence to be the murderer of a child. The circumstantial case is compelling to the policeman, but it would not be compelling in a court of law. The policeman decides that he will beat a confession out of the murderer, which he proceeds to do. After several hours of various forms of torture, the murderer confesses. This is not a false confession but a true one that is substantiated by material evidence that the murderer discloses to the policeman as a result of the beating. What should be the consequences for the offender? Under our constitutional system the integrity of procedure would free the murderer, assuming that the material evidence obtained through torture was necessary for a conviction. It would not be an answer to argue that the murderer ought to be punished and so should the policeman who beat the confession out of him. The policeman was not merely assaulting the murderer, he was gathering evidence. From a strictly consequentialist or utilitarian perspective, the murderer should not go free, since he threatens the entire community. Yet a community with our historical principles of criminal justice may not enforce law based on the crimes of its agents.

It is often very hard to accept the implications of a principled approach to punishment. I have purposely begun my discussion with an extreme and relatively easy example. Whatever one's attitude toward the exclusionary rule (which I shall discuss later), it seems unlikely that any theory, pro- or anti-utilitarian, would support a legal system that accepted evidence arising out of torture. I have used that example to suggest some of the harder issues testing the integrity of the criminal justice system: lying during criminal investigations or interrogations, the exclusionary rule of evidence, sentencing, and corrections.

Investigation and Deception

Suppose I were to address the just deserts advocate as follows: Assuming that we would agree that the police should not be permitted to torture suspects, should they be permitted to lie to them? To be consistent, a principled anti-utilitarian would have to acknowledge that since lying is morally impermissible, it should not be allowed as a routine feature of law enforcement. Yet in fact, when police officers are investigating crimes, not only are they allowed to lie, trick, and deceive, but they are expected to do so. Indeed, one might properly conclude, from examining police practices subjected to the highest appellate review, that police are authoritatively encouraged to lie. Detectives, for example, are trained to use informers or to act themselves as informers or agents provocateurs when the criminal activities under investigation involve possession or sale of contraband, whether counterfeit money, stolen goods, or drugs. All enforcement strategies involving contraband are effective only when they employ enormous amounts of deception.

The utilitarianism of deception raises questions about the consistency of those who advocate a just deserts rationale as the principal goal of law enforcement. Is it really possible to reconcile a punishment system grounded on the idea of justice with investigative lying?

The idea of entrapment is, of course, an illustration of an attempt to reconcile integrity with deception within the law enforcement system. We may not use evidence of crime against someone who has been "entrapped" into committing the forbidden act. Yet from my reading of the law, the definition of entrapment is rather hazy. One, the subjective approach, focuses upon the background, character, and intention of the defendant. Is he or she the sort of person who would be predisposed to commit the crime, even without the participation of the government official or agent? The other test, the objective one, sets its sights on the nature of the governmental participation. Since the subjective test focuses upon the defendant, the conduct of the government agent ordinarily would have much more latitude.

The subjective test of entrapment permits lying when it does not encourage the criminality of the defendant. Thus, in the leading entrapment case, *United States* v. *Russell,* Justice Rehnquist and a majority of the Court held that the defendant was not entrapped by a federal drug agent posing as an illegal drug seller because he had been an active participant in an illegal drug manufacturing enterprise that began before the government agent appeared on the scene and continued after the government left the scene.[6] Russell was described in the case as an "unwary criminal" rather than an "unwary innocent." The subjective test, in short, permits the police to lie provided that the deception catches a wolf rather than a lamb. Actually, both legal tests of entrapment, the subjective and the objective, permit police to employ an enormous amount of routine lying, although the prevailing subjective test permits more.

Yet the truthfulness demanded by the objective test is not very clear either. Justice Frankfurter presented the objective test as follows: "The crucial question, not easy to answer, to which the Court must direct itself, is whether the police conduct revealed in the particular case falls below standards, to which common feeling responds, for the proper use of governmental power."[7] The objective test seems to conceive of significant limitations on police conduct in the interest of maintaining a civilized or moral constabulary. Thus, to return to my earlier example, a civilized police force should not be permitted to torture suspects to obtain confessions, even when the background, character, and intention of the suspects indicate serious criminality. Nor, to cite a real case, would moral police be permitted to pump the stomach of a suspected narcotics dealer to show that the pills he had just swallowed contained morphine, even if that is exactly what the pills did contain.

Such concepts as common feelings or the conscience of the community arguably imply enduring and stable values. But do they in reality? Arguably, not only do they vary cross-culturally, they vary temporally within a given community or nation. Common feelings might allow for far more latitude in police practices during periods of high fear of crimes. Moreover, consider that even in the dissenting opinion in *Russell,* Justice Stewart, supporting the objective test, wrote that "the government's use of undercover activity, strategy, or deception is not necessarily unlawful. Indeed, many crimes, especially so-called victimless crimes, could not otherwise be detected."[8] Here we see an illustration of the objective test yielding entirely to a utilitarian justification. Thus, judicial permissiveness regarding investigative deception suggests how difficult it is to defend, even in the abstract, a principled imperative against lying; and how it would be for any such defense to be accepted by courts, police, and the public. Courts permit similar sorts of deception during the interrogation stage of the process, although forbidding it during testimony.

I have argued elsewhere that judicial acceptance of deception by detectives during the investigation and interrogation stages encourages deception during trial—perjury—on precisely the sort of utilitarian justification the courts employ to permit lying during investigation. Thus, on utilitarian grounds the police officer may feel morally justified in lying in court (for example, about how evidence was obtained) to demonstrate the truth of the larger issue of whether the accused is guilty. No one, of course, would suggest that police officers' lying at trial is consistent with principled law enforcement. Yet the system encourages police lying before trial. Deception by police surely challenges us to consider the limits of the integrity of the retributive ideal.

Integrity and the Exclusionary Rule

The exclusionary rule is possibly the most widely discussed issue in criminal procedure. The rule was originally based on the idea that the government should not benefit from official misconduct. It is thus the principal systemic bulwark upholding integrity throughout the guilt determination process. The exclusionary rule says that the government cannot use evidence obtained in violation of constitutional guarantees against unreasonable searches and seizures. The rule was first announced in *Weeks* v. *United States* (1914) and originally was limited to federal courts.[9] In a recent symposium on the exclusionary rule, the editors note that the rule did not provoke public discussion until it was extended to state courts, since the state courts deal with the great majority of violent crimes and thus tend to be the focal point of citizen interest.[10] That is not entirely accurate. By the time the Court extended the rule in *Mapp* v. *Ohio* in 1961, half of the American states had adopted it. Of these, twenty appear to have adopted it without substantial qualification.[11] Thus, California had adopted the exclusionary rule in 1955, and that adoption, in an opinion written by Justice Traynor, was influential and controversial.[12] William H. Parker, then the police chief of Los Angeles, protested that the decision was a terrible blow to law enforcement, conceivably setting law enforcement back fifty years. Nevertheless, by the time the Supreme Court handed down its decision in *Mapp* v. *Ohio,* of the populous states besides Ohio, only New York had not adopted the exclusionary rule. So although *Mapp* v. *Ohio* could be said technically to have imposed the exclusionary rule on the states, in fact it imposed it only on half the states.

There are two justifications behind the exclusionary rule, one utilitarian and the other principled. The utilitarian rationale argues that just as criminal law is supposed to deter potential criminals, the exclusionary rule will aid in preventing broad warrantless searches by police. The assumptions behind the deterrence rationale were stated most clearly by Justice Traynor when the exclusionary rule was adopted in 1955 in California: "Granted that the adoption of the exclusionary rule will not prevent all illegal searches and seizures, it will discourage them. Police officers and prosecuting officials are primarily interested in convicting criminals. Given the exclusionary rule and the choice between securing evidence by legal rather than illegal means, officers will be impelled to obey the law themselves, since not to do so will jeopardize their objectives."[13]

There have been several (in my opinion inconclusive) studies regarding the impact of the exclusionary rule, one of which I conducted myself.[14] It is worth noting, however, in regard to the previous discussion of police deception, one of the early responses to the exclusionary rule for New York police: they perjured themselves about how they collected evidence. Such lies came to be known as "dropsie" testimony. The police testified that those charged with drug possession were now dropping illicit drugs on the ground where police could find them rather than keeping them hidden on their person.[15] Prior to that, evidence obtained from such unlawful searches of the person was, of course, admissable. Thus, the police didn't have to lie to achieve the objective to which Justice Traynor alluded in his 1955 California decision. They were illegal but truthful. After *Mapp* they continued to be illegal in the searching and seizing practices, but they lied about their illegality. Some commentators have employed this illustration to support a glaring non sequitur: the example shows how ineffective the exclusionary rule is in deterring police conduct; therefore, we should abandon it.

The deterrence rationale has little to do with the other strand of justification, namely the integrity rationale. Professor Yale Kamisar has been perhaps the most articulate and vigorous spokesperson for the integrity rationale. As he wrote in a recent article, "The exclusion of reliable evidence does impose a 'cost' on society, but so do unreasonable searches and seizures—and the perception, by the public and the police alike, that our courts do not take seriously the constitutional protection against such police misconduct."[16] The exclusionary principle is an essential aspect of the integrity of our punishment system. Any principled justification for punishment must include exclusion of evidence obtained through governmental misconduct. Nor is it true, as Chief Justice Burger has claimed, that the exclusionary rule is "unique to American jurisprudence,"[17] or that, as Judge Malcolm Wilkey has argued, "one proof of the irrationality of the exclusionary rule is that no other civilized nation has adopted it."[18] Walter Pakter, who has recently completed a comparative study of the rule, points out that an exclusionary rule existed in France and Germany even before it was introduced in America, and that the role of exclusion has been expanding in France, Germany, and Italy during the past thirty years.[19]

The exclusionary rule was recently limited by the Supreme Court in *United States* v. *Leon*.[20] Under *Leon*'s "good-faith" exception, evidence collected under a warrant will not be excluded on the basis of an appellate court's subsequent decision that probable cause for the warrant was insufficient as long as the police officer did not mislead the magistrate through intentional or reckless disregard for the truth. The impact of *Leon* on the integrity of the criminal justice system remains to be seen. The "good-faith" exception might be defensible from a principled retributive perspective insofar as public confidence in the system's integrity may be undermined when criminals escape punishment not because of lawless police activity but because of confusing law that leaves even the earnest police officer without a guideline.

The standard of *Leon* seems, however, neither to eliminate the exclusionary rule nor to reward police lawlessness. It does not even reward the blundering constable. Under such a standard, a police officer must act prudently enough to be able to persuade a court that his mistake was reasonable. The good-faith standard should put a burden on police to know the laws protecting the constitutional rights of citizens and to be responsive to those rights. An untrained officer should not be able to claim a reasonable good-faith mistake. Moreover, the standard almost by definition cannot offer police more than one bite at the apple of a given good-faith mistake. Police scarcely could say in good faith that they made the same mistake twice.

The integrity of the good-faith standard clearly would demand careful judicial scrutiny of police claims made under it, and that is the rub. One criticism of the exclusionary rule in the past has been that judges have been pushed toward dangerously expanded notions of the legality of search in order to admit evidence that they are reluctant to suppress. Judges could also undermine a reasonable good-faith standard, and might do so in practice. There is no getting around the need for judicial integrity—without it, a good-faith exception would be an abysmal failure. If police take the *Leon* decision as an invitation to seek out "rubber-stamp" magistrates to validate searches and arrests they know are unlawful, and the courts uphold this, the exception may prove an irreparable blow to the system's integrity.[21]

The Consistency of Punishment

The integrity of the retributive ideal would seem to call for both propriety in evidence gathering and consistency of certain rules of punishment. Retribution—just deserts—implies two principles, proportionality and invariability. Neither principle is easily achieved in practice, further undermining our capacity to maintain the integrity of the retributive ideal. Let us consider some of the difficulties: first, if the idea of just deserts has, as Andrew von Hirsch suggests, "its counterpart in common sense notions of equity which people apply in their everyday lives,"[22] we may find that such notions vary according to standard social attributes such as education, income, geography, and ethnicity. Moreover, we may wish to distinguish between carefully reasoned notions of equity and unconsidered expressions of anger and resentment.

I am reminded of Judge Marvin Frankel's decision in *United States v. Bergman*.[23] Bergman had appeared to be a man of unimpeachably high character, attainments, and distinction. However, investigations of nursing homes suggested that he, among others, was collecting on fraudulent claims for Medicaid funds. Bergman pleaded guilty to a conspiracy to defraud, and Frankel was faced with the task of sentencing him. Bergman—sixty-four years old and in less than perfect health—was sentenced by Judge Frankel to four months' imprisonment for his crime. "For all but the proudly vengeful," wrote Judge Frankel, "it [the sentence] should not depreciate the seriousness of his offenses." But I suppose it would not surprise anyone to learn that the sentence of four months' imprisonment was highly criticized by New York newspapers for its leniency. Apparently, the newspapers and Judge Frankel held different "common sense" standards of equity.

Other New York judges might have agreed—or disagreed—with Judge Frankel's reasoning. Even if they had agreed, consider the potential for variation built into our federal system. The differing penalty structures already prevailing in different states argue against an easy assumption of across-the-board notions of equity, aside from the influence of social and personality factors.

I have perhaps already misled the reader by suggesting that judicial sentencing is more important than plea bargaining ("the exchange of official concessions for the act of self-conviction") in influencing variations in punishment. Plea bargaining, as Malcolm Feeley has pointed out, covers a broad spectrum of negotiated outcomes in the criminal justice process.[24] It probably accounts for more variation in sentencing than does judicial pronouncement. By itself, it seriously challenges the aspiration to uniformity implicit in the just desert ideal. Not only do different prosecutors, like judges, entertain differing notions of just desert, they negotiate for different reasons and under different pressures. Moreover, even if plea bargaining were to be eliminated, prosecutors would retain enough discretion at the charging level to cast doubt on the uniformity of just deserts.

Conceptual difficulties challenge the retributive model as well. Even if we could assume general agreement among all judges or prosecutors on what punishment a particular criminal deserves, we would not have resolved the problem of proportionality. Criminal acts do not fall on an interval or ratio scale the way such variables as age and income do. A forty-year-old person is twice twenty, and $15,000 is a third of $45,000. Crimes fall at best on an ordinal (better or worse) scale—that is, robbery is clearly worse than burglary, but it cannot be said to be twice or

1.4 times as bad. To complicate matters further, crimes do not always fall on an ordinal scale—who is worse, the drug seller or the burglar? The proportionality concept often suggested by just deserts advocates—based on a ratio assumption—suggests a relational precision that simply doesn't occur in reality.

Invariance is the second just deserts principle. According to von Hirsch, the integrity of the deserts principle "is infringed when disparate separate penalties are imposed on equally deserving offenders. If *A* and *B* commit a burglary under circumstances suggesting similar culpability, they deserve similar punishments."[25] But the idea of similar punishment is also elusive. Variation always means a difference from something, but writers sometimes confuse moral with statistical variation. One example cited in the sentencing literature involves a defendant convicted for possession of marijuana and sentenced to six months in jail.[26] In the same jurisdiction a second defendant is found guilty of possessing an illegal weapon and sentenced to thirty days. Commentator A feels that these sentences are disparate because the offender committing the more serious and dangerous crime received a less severe sanction. By contrast, commentator B points out that it would be possible to analyze a large sample of cases in the jurisdiction and find that everyone convicted of possessing marijuana receives a sentence of six months, while everyone convicted of possessing an illegal weapon receives a sentence of thirty days. Commentator A is confusing justice with variation. Statistically speaking, the sentences are not variant.

The statistical vision of variation, however, suggests other problems. When researchers look at large numbers of sentences or the setting of terms by parole boards, they characteristically find general statistical patterns in which there is some variation from established norms. Problems exist in both conceptualizing variation and deciding where it is acceptable. Martin Forst points out that one way to draw the line between acceptable and unacceptable variation is with absolute time. But, as he further shows, absolute time does not allow for consideration of the relative lengths of the sentences imposed. A variation of six months for an average robbery sentence of twenty years is not very much. In contrast, a variation of six months for two pickpockets, one of whom is sentenced to six months in jail and the other to one year, is considerable.

Alternatively, one could define disparity in relative terms as a specific percentage or proportion above or below the central tendency of a predicted sentence. But if we use qualitative concepts such as slight, moderate, and great, would we say that a 10 percent variation is slight, moderate, or great? How about 5 percent or 20 percent? There is no way of scientifically defining the defining acceptability of variation. We can, of course, be reasonably confident that prisoners will tend to perceive variation more narrowly than will outside observers. In any case, variation and disproportion are problems that must be considered from the moral perspective of the retributivist, and rarely are.[27]

Punishment

If the concept of just deserts perplexes us in the sentencing process, it is even more vexing when we turn our attention to the punishment end of the criminal justice system. What sort of punishment is acceptable to the retributive ideal? Harsh and abusive treatment of prisoners is nothing new. Prisoners have always been subjected to a variety of abuses, legal and extralegal, from being physically brutalized or medically neglected to being forced to remain silent and to walk in lockstep. They have been subjected to racial discrimination, chain gangs, rigid censorship, restricted visitation rights, even torture. In the face of this history, how are we to decide which punishments are consistent with the integrity of the retributive ideal? More important, if we decide that a punishment is not permissible, what is the remedy?

The Constitution sets a vague outer limit for the notion of permissible punishment. The Eighth Amendment is supposed to assure that the state's punishing power is exercised within the limits of civilized standards, and it "must draw its meaning from the evolving standards of decency that mark the progress of a maturing society."[28] At present, three principal tests determine whether a prison's regimen violates the strictures of the Eighth Amendment: Does the punishment shock the general conscience of a civilized society? Is the punishment unnecessarily cruel? And does the punishment go beyond legitimate penal aims? Certain specific practices or conditions have been held to constitute a system of cruel and unusual punishment. Among those violating the Eighth Amendment are "overcrowding, inadequate medical treatment, physical abuse by guards, solitary confinement in strip cells or for excessive periods of time, lack of outdoor exercise or recreation, inadequate diet, and almost all forms of corporal punishment."[29]

Despite the affirmative recognition of prisoners' rights, the courts are nevertheless limited in their capacity to deliver on those rights. A court is a reasonably good instrument for settling a dispute between two contending parties. It may not be so qualified to oversee and reform the activities of a variety of social institutions, such as prisons, mental hospitals, and school systems. As a result, judicial recognition of prisoners' rights may be more significant as symbol than as substance.

Let me offer the *Little* v. *Walker* (1977)[30] case as vivid illustration. Little was an inmate at the Illinois state penitentiary in Stateville. He filed a civil rights class action alleging that he and other inmates at Stateville "repeatedly suffered acts and threats of physical violence, sexual assaults, and other crimes perpetrated by other inmates from whom plaintiffs were not reasonably protected by defendants." Little and those who joined him in his suit said that they lived in constant and imminent fear of physical violence and sexual assault, especially from gang-affiliated inmates. To avoid the violence and assaults, Little and his fellow plaintiffs asked to be put into protective segregation.

According to the decision of the court of appeals the prison authorities apparently made no distinction between disciplinary and protective segregation. Those placed in protective segregation were housed next to the most violence-prone inmates in the institution. Inmates in the segregation safekeeping status had meals served to them in their cells by gang-affiliated inmates who "withheld meals from plaintiffs unless plaintiffs performed unnatural sexual acts through the cell bars." Moreover, the cell house where the segregation safekeeping inmates were housed was taken over by a group of rebellious inmates for nine hours while gang rapes were inflicted on the other inmates, whose personal property was also destroyed and confiscated.

The court had no difficulty in finding that the violent attacks and sexual assaults on the plaintiff while in protective segregation were manifestly "inconsistent with contemporary standards of decency." That is, even though Little himself was a criminal assigned to a maximum security prison, his punishment never should have included this sort of "unnecessary and wanton infliction of pain." There is no doubt that the conditions of Stateville Prison violated the constitutional rights of the prisoners under the Eighth Amendment. The prison was placed under court order requiring that officials remedy the situation.

In the abstract, the system was vindicated—it appeared to have integrity—because the courts had acted. But what difference did that make? James Jacobs, who has written a notable sociological study of

Stateville,[31] argues elsewhere that although it is difficult to assess compliance with court decrees, on the whole prisoners' rights have been implemented by court decrees because a declaration of rights symbolically upholds constitutional principles.[32] Other students of judicial impact also tend to be on the optimistic side, although all recognize the limitations of such equitable judgments and the difficulties of evaluating their impact.[33] As to the latter, it is instructive to compare Jacobs's optimism with a later description of Stateville. Jacobs wrote in 1980: "In 1975, at Stateville, there was only a handful of medical personnel. In 1979, the Illinois Department of Corrections and Prison Legal Services signed a consent decree which called for a medical staff of forty-eight persons (Cook v. Rowe, No. 76 C 2224, N.D. Ill. 1979). Care is to be provided around the clock and includes the services of medical technicians stationed in each cell house, fully qualified nurses, a half-dozen dentists, several doctors, a physical therapist, and an X-ray technician."[34]

By contrast, Kevin Krojick offers a very different and far bleaker picture of the prison. Krojick describes the results of a ten-year battle to control the institution. This struggle, he found, left the prison "a hellhole for both inmates and staff." Rapes and stabbings were almost daily events, and piles of feces and garbage stood knee-deep in some spots. However important symbolic court victories are, one has to wonder at their lasting impact on the treatment of the individual offender. Nearly a year and a half later, an uneasy silence reigned at Stateville. Authorities had been able to reduce violence and gang control substantially. Basic services were being delivered. But the prison was still far too crowded. Almost a third of the inmates were idle, and there were no concrete plans to provide them with jobs.[35]

Which evaluation of Stateville are we to believe? Actually, Jacobs's and Krojick's evaluations are not contradictory. Jacobs is discussing the narrow issue of the impact of a consent decree on medical services, while Krojick is examining the prison as a whole. Krojick's description seems to capture the overall reality of the prison better (as does Jacobs's book). Stateville is probably not the worst of our maximum security prisons and surely is not the best. It may not be unusual, but it is cruel for many inmates.

We also can predict confidently that conditions in our prisons are worsening since they are becoming more crowded. According to a prison population survey at the end of 1983, the United States experienced a sharp increase in prison population in the early 1980s. At the end of 1983, federal and state correctional facilities held 438,830 persons.[36] "This figure," according to Austin and Krisberg, "means that the nation's prison population had doubled during the last decade and had become the largest in U.S. history."[37] These increases probably occurred because of the widespread adoption of new laws that mandated prison sentences for certain offenses and in general lengthened prison terms. The result has been serious overcrowding. Prisons are also very expensive. It costs upwards of $50,000 per bed to build a high-security facility. Under the sort of conditions we have discussed at Stateville, the potential for uprisings exists in more than a few state institutions.

In *Chapman* v. *Rhodes*, the U.S. Supreme Court was asked to rule whether doubling up of inmates in cells designed for one was "cruel and unusual punishment."[38] The prison in question was an Ohio maximum security prison which was hailed as a model for such institutions. After reviewing the overall conditions of the prison, the Supreme Court found (June 15, 1981) that, taking all the circumstances into account, double celling did not inflict "unnecessary or wanton pain," nor was it "grossly disproportionate to the severity of crimes warranting imprisonment," the two tests the Court has come to rely upon as indexes of cruel and unusual punishment.

But however the Court ruled, it would not have resolved the underlying dilemma: the more people we imprison, and for longer terms, the more overcrowded our prisons become. The more overcrowded they become, the more likely it is that the conditions will worsen. Moreover, given that double celling is now constitutionally permitted, it is unlikely that states will be moved to build new prison space. But if they don't, how will they deal with the worsening threat of prison violence and decay? If double celling had been found to be unconstitutional and the states were required to build more prisons, how would we force them? Where would they put the prisons and how would they afford them? In reality, there is no way to reconcile the current interpretation of retribution prevailing in state legislatures (and among some scholars as well) with the integrity inhering in the retributive ideal. We can't lock people up and treat them as animals in the name of just deserts. In reality we seem less concerned with the justice of desert than with long-term incapacitation. Courts may offer some remedy for the excesses resulting from grossly inadequate prison facilities, but their capacity is severely strained as sentences grow and public budgets decline.

Selective Incapacitation

As a result of prison overcrowding and the fear of crime we are increasingly being led to consider utilitarian schemes to relieve the tensions created by acting on the impulse to be retributive. Take, for example, the idea of selective incapacitation, proposed by Peter W. Greenwood (with Allan Abrahamse) of the Rand Corporation.[39] The theory of selective incapacitation is based partly on the assumption (derived from previous research) that most offenders commit relatively few crimes, while a handful commit many crimes. Their theory is also based on the assumption that, because of limited prison space, offenders on the average will spend less time in prison than the public wants them to.

Selective incapacitation thus proposes to identify and "select" high-risk offenders and imprison them—that is, incapacitate them—for a substantial period of time beyond what they would normally serve. Since the really threatening culprits would thus be identified, the overwhelming majority of prisoners could be released earlier, making the justice system more equitable and cutting its costs. Greenwood's proposal is intriguing and closely reasoned. But not only is it probably too good to be true, it is surely utilitarian.

The selective incapacitation scheme was developed from the results of a questionnaire given to 2,190 inmates in California, Michigan, and Texas who had been convicted of robbery and burglary. The researchers were not able to study murderers and sex offenders because too few turned up in the sample to permit statistical analysis. Some of the robbers and burglars (from 10 percent to 60 percent, depending on the institution) did not complete the questionnaire.

The respondents were asked to recount their criminal careers. The authors are confident that these inmates were truthful about reporting criminal conduct that was not known to authorities. What is the evidence for this? "Visual inspection of the survey booklets and the field reports of the administrators," wrote the authors, "suggests that most inmates were trying to provide accurate information." Other checks were also employed, but one still has to remain skeptical.

By cross-tabulating various predictors against self-reports of offenders, the authors selected seven factors to make up the prediction scale: Had the offender been incarcerated for more than twelve months during the two years preceding the most recent offense? Had he used heroin or drugs during that period? Was he employed for less than half of that time? Was he convicted before for the same crime? Was he convicted of an offense before he was sixteen? Was he incarcerated in a state or federal juvenile facility? Did he use drugs as a juvenile?

The respondents were given one point for a positive response to any of these seven variables. According to the authors' predictions, if the inmate scored 4 or higher he would be a real bad guy when released; a 2 or 3 was rated medium-bad; and a 0 to 1 was not so bad at all.

Notice that the variables do not deal directly with race or socioeconomic status. Several of them are clearly race sensitive, however. The unemployment rate for black juveniles has been more than twice that for whites. The authors were aware of this problem and tried to eliminate some of these items, but then the scale didn't work.

I see several problems in the proposal. First, by avoiding racial and socioeconomic variables, the authors may have eliminated, solely on ethical and constitutional grounds, the very best predictive terms. Couldn't an offender identified as a high risk claim that he is entitled to the most scientific predictors, whether or not they jibe with the researchers' social views? This seems to be a Catch-22: The use of such racial criteria could well be found unconstitutional, yet their absence might well lead to less scientifically valid results.

Second, I question any predictive scheme that assumes consistent linear development of human beings. Most adolescents commit illegal acts. In the case of some, criminal behavior will increase; for others, it will decline. People change as they age. This scheme offers predictions based on self-reported past criminality but does not and cannot test the future.

Finally, the inevitability of false positives—people inaccurately identified as high-risk offenders—bedevils any statistical prediction scheme. Let us assume that the proposed scale is 90 percent accurate. (Since the scale hasn't been tested, nobody knows its unconditional accuracy. Given, however, the uncertainty of offender-based data, an assumption of 90 percent accuracy would be quite generous.) Next, the researchers estimate that out of every 1,000 inmates, about 50 will be high-risk offenders.

Based on these assumptions, my calculations show: Out of the 50 true high-risk offenders, 45 will properly be identified as such, and 5 will be falsely labeled as low risk. Out of the 950 actual low-risk offenders, 855 will be identified that way, and 95 will be inaccurately labeled as high risks. Thus, 140 of the 1,000 will be identified as high risks. In fact, only 45 of the 140 identified actually are. Therefore, the sentences of 95 low-risk offenders will have been unjustly extended by a false prediction.

How did a scale that we estimated was 90 percent accurate become only 32 percent accurate? Statisticians label this transformation conditional probability. The accuracy of a predictor depends upon the distribution or base rate of the predicted phenomenon. Conditional probability may prove to be the undoing of selective incapacitation.[40]

Other Rand researchers, Jan and Marcia Chaiken, are also critical of selective incapacitation. Like Greenwood, they are in the business of trying to distinguish the worst offenders. But they are well aware of the limits of self-report data and regression analyses for predicting future criminality. Moreover, they argue, "Even if the models were foolproof, the legal and ethical ramifications of their use by the criminal justice system would be a matter of dispute. Sentencing offenders for past crimes that have never been adjudicated runs counter to the principle of just deserts, while sentencing them for predicted future crimes runs counter to tenets of free will and justice. Therefore, we suggest that our findings should not be used simplistically as criteria for passing judgment on specific individuals."[41] In sum, they argue that a sentencing system loses integrity when offenders are incapacitated for self-reported past crimes or predicted future ones.

The Debasement of the Retributive Ideal

Faced with rising crime rates, fiscal limitations, and a fearful public, legislators have imposed increasingly lengthy and mandatory sentences throughout the United States. They have also deemphasized rehabilitation as a goal of the criminal justice system, partly out of a widely held misunderstanding of the research on rehabilitation.

Under indeterminate sentencing systems that developed throughout the United States, the rehabilitative ideal was more often debased than practiced. Treatment lapsed into custody, and training into makework.[42]

It is also possible, I have argued here, to debase the retributive ideal.

Those who believe in the retributive ideal—an ideal of justice—must face the realities of contemporary law enforcement. If we are to achieve just retribution, we cannot blind ourselves to enforcement realities from arrest through conviction. It is not enough to proclaim an ideal as an aspiration. My sociological instincts—or biases—press me toward examination of realistic outcomes. If these undermine, even debase, well-intentioned aspirations, it might be wiser to try to understand why that happens, rather than to continue to proclaim the aspiration. The insistence upon a debased ideal is sheer hypocrisy. No one should claim justice in that.

Notes

1. See Francis A. Allen, *The Decline of the Rehabilitative Ideal: Penal Policy and Social Purpose* (New Haven and London: Yale University Press, 1981).
2. J. J. C. Smart and Bernard Williams, *Utilitarianism: For and Against* (Cambridge: Cambridge University Press, 1973), pp. 116–17.
3. Thomas Nagel, "Ruthlessness in Public Life," in *Public and Private Morality*, ed. Stuart Hampshire (New York: Cambridge University Press, 1978), pp. 75–92.
4. *Mapp* v. *Ohio*, 367 U.S. 643 (1961).
5. H. L. A. Hart, *Punishment and Responsibility: Essays in the Philosophy of Law* (New York: Oxford University Press, 1968), p. 7.
6. *United States* v. *Russell*, 411 U.S. 423 (1973).
7. *Sherman* v. *United States*, 356 U.S. 369 at 383 (1958), Frankfurter concurring.
8. *United States* v. *Russell*, 32 id. at 445, Stewart dissenting. Cf. also Jerome Skolnick, "Deception by Police," *Criminal Justice Ethics* 1, no. 2 (Summer/Fall 1982): 40–54.
9. *Weeks* v. *United States*, 232 U.S. 383 (1914).
10. "Symposium on the Exclusionary Rule," *Criminal Justice Ethics* 1, no. 2 (Summer/Fall 1982): 4–40.
11. *Mapp* v. *Ohio*, 367 U.S. 643 (1961).
12. *People* v. *Cahan*, 44 Cal. 2d 434 (1955).
13. Id., at 448.
14. Illustrative studies include: Jerome Skolnick, *Justice without Trial*, 2d ed. (New York: J. C. Wiley and Sons, 1975), pp. 211–19; Dallin H. Oaks, "Studying the Exclusionary Rule in Search and Seizure," *University of Chicago Law Review* 37 (1980): 37; Stephen Schlesinger, "The Exclusionary Rule: Have Proponents Proven That It Is a Deterrent to Police?" *Judicature* 62 (1979): 404; Milton Loew-

enthal, "Evaluating the Exclusionary Rule in Search and Seizure," *University of Missouri-Kansas City Law Review* 49 (1980): 38.

15. Oaks, "Studying the Exclusionary Rule."

16. Yale Kamisar, "Does (Did) (Should) the Exclusionary Rule Rest on a 'Principled Basis' Rather than an Empirical Proposition?" *Creighton Law Review* 16 (Summer 1982–83): 565–667.

17. *Bivens* v. *Six Unknown Unnamed Agents of the Federal Bureau of Narcotics*, 403 U.S. 388 (1971), Burger dissenting.

18. Richard Malcolm Wilkey, "The Exclusionary Rule: Why Suppress Evidence," *Judicature* 62 (1978): 216.

19. Walter Pakter, "*The Exclusionary Rule: A Comparative Study,*" manuscript presented to faculty colloquium, March 4, 1983, Boalt Hall, University of California, Berkeley.

20. *United States* v. *Leon*, 468 U.S. 897, 104 S. Ct. 3405 (1984).

21. Candace McCoy, "The Good-Faith Warrant Cases—What Price Judge-Shopping?" *Criminal Law Bulletin* 21 (1985): 53. On the other hand, insofar as *Leon* takes some of the pressure off judges to compromise substantive Fourth Amendment rules in order to avoid exclusion in situations of technical errors by police or magistrates it will provide considerable benefit. In an earlier case, *Illinois* v. *Gates*, 462 U.S. 213, 103 S. Ct. 2317 (1983), the Court adopted a less restrictive definition of probable cause in order to prevent exclusion of evidence gathered in the execution of a search warrant rather than employing a "good-faith" exception proposed in a concurring opinion by Justice White, who later gathered the majority opinion in *Leon*.

22. Andrew von Hirsch, "Doing Justice: The Principle of Commensurate Deserts," in Hyman Gross and Andrew von Hirsch, *Sentencing* (New York: Oxford University Press, 1981), p. 244.

23. *United States* v. *Bergman*, 416 F. Supp. 496 (S.D.N.Y. 1976).

24. Malcolm M. Feeley, "Perspectives on Plea Bargaining," *Law and Society Review* 13 (1979): 199.

25. Von Hirsch, "Doing Justice," p. 247.

26. Martin L. Forst, "Sentencing Disparity: An Overview of Research and Issues," in *Sentencing Reform: Experiments in Reducing Disparity*, Sage Criminal Justice System Annuals, vol. 17, ed. Martin L. Forst (Beverly Hills: Sage Publications, 1982), pp. 9–34.

27. One source of variation through the results of negotiated guilty pleas are problems of inadmissable evidence which may force the prosecution to agree to lower charges. Integrity at one stage can undermine integrity at a later stage.

28. *Trop* v. *Dulles*, 356 U.S. 86 at 100–101 (1958).

29. Alvin J. Bronstein, "Prisoners' Rights: A History," in *Legal Rights of Prisoners*,

Sage Criminal Justice System Annuals, vol. 14, ed. Geoffrey P. Alpert (Beverly Hills: Sage Publications, 1980), p. 27.

30. *Little* v. *Walker*, 552 F.2d 193 97th Cir. (1977).

31. James B. Jacobs, *Stateville: The Penitentiary in Mass Society* (Chicago: University of Chicago Press, 1977).

32. James B. Jacobs, "The Prisoners' Rights Movement and Its Impacts, 1960–1980," in *Crime and Justice: An Annual Review of Research*, vol. 2, ed. Norval Morris and Michael Tonry (Chicago: University of Chicago Press, 1980), pp. 429–70.

33. Probably the cleanest measure of the impact of court decrees on improving prisons is simply to observe whether the changes ordered have actually been made. Did Stateville really hire the medical staff the judge demanded? Were vocational programs ordered for other prisons really instituted? The most familiar example of this type of impact study is M. Kay Harris and D. P. Spiller, *After Decision: Implementation of Judicial Decrees in Correctional Settings* (Washington, D.C.: U.S. Department of Justice, L.E.A.A., 1977). Harris and Spiller concluded that litigation forced prison administrators to clean up the very worst prison conditions (vermin, corporal punishment, gross overcrowding), but that it did no more than to raise institutional quality slightly above minimally humane living standards. Other studies conclude that the weight of litigation itself caused prison administrators to institute new programs; in these cases, grievance procedures or ombudsman programs were started. Administrators hoped that if prisoners had a meaningful outlet for venting their complaints within the prison walls, the frustration of outside litigation would be avoided. Candace McCoy, "The Impact of Section 1983 Litigation on Corrections Policymaking," *Federal Probation* 18 (Dec. 1981): 18.

Grievance procedures indicate to the prisoner that he or she is a human being whose story will be heard, and as such they touch on Bronstein's observation that prisoners' rights litigation is at base an affirmation of the humanity of the convict. "Without respect," he said, "human rights are meaningless" ("Prisoners' Right," p. 19). The "optimistic" commentators maintain that mechanical compliance with court orders should not be the measure of the impact of corrections litigation; the true impact is evident in changes symbolically upholding the human dignity of the incarcerated or in political realignments set into motion by the litigation. "Such 'secondary effects' include the organization of prisoners, citizen and interest group mobilization, legislative and budgetmaking decisions and lawmaking, professional standard-setting, and the redistribution of power inside the prisons" (Jacobs, "Prisoners' Rights Movement," p. 454). These effects are quite difficult to measure empirically. Some have tried: A. Champagne and K. C. Haas, "The Impact of *Johnson* v. *Avery* on Prison Administration," *Tennessee Law Review* 43 (1976): 275; Sol Rubin, "The Impact of Court Decisions on the Correctional Process," *Crime and Delinquency* 20 (1974): 129–34. For an argument that the major impact is a psychological one—the prisoners' perception that they are valuable people who have rights and can organize to demand them—see Stuart A. Scheingold, *The Politics of Rights* (New Haven: Yale University Press, 1974).

34. Jacobs, "Prisoners' Rights Movement," pp. 464–65.

35. Kevin Krojick, "At Stateville, the Calm is Tense," *Corrections Magazine* 6, no. 3 (June 1980): 6.

36. *Prisoners in 1983*, Bureau of Justice Statistics Bulletin (Washington, D.C.: Department of Justice, BJS, 1984), app. A.

37. J. Austin and B. Krisberg, "Incarceration in the United States: The Extent and Future of the Problem," *Annals of the American Academy of Political and Social Science* 478 (March 1985): 15–30.

38. *Chapman* v. *Rhodes,* 101 S. Ct. 2392 (1981).

39. Peter W. Greenwood, with Allan Abrahamse, *Selective Incapacitation,* Publication R-2815-NIJ (Santa Monica: The Rand Corporation, 1982).

40. Cf. John Blackmore and Jane Welsh, "Selective Incapacitation: Sentencing According to Risk," *Crime and Delinquency* 29, no. 4 (Oct 1983): 504–28; Andrew von Hirsch and Don M. Gottfredson, "Selective Incapacitation: Some Queries about Research Design and Equity," *N.Y.U. Review of Law and Social Change* 12, no. 1 (1983–84): 11–52.

41. Jan M. Chaiken and Marcia M. Chaiken, *Varieties of Criminal Behavior: Summary and Policy Implications,* Publication R-2814-NIJ (Santa Monica: The Rand Corporation, 1981).

42. Allen, *The Decline of the Rehabilitative Ideal.*

Beyond Rehabilitation

AUSTIN D. SARAT

Let prisons and prison systems be lighted by the law of love. Let us leave, for the present, the thought of inflicting punishment upon prisoners to satisfy so-called justice and turn toward the reformation of criminals.

Zebulan Brockway, warden of the Detroit House of Correction, before the Congress of the American Prison Association, 1870

Persons convicted of crime shall be dealt with in accordance with their potential for rehabilitation, considering their individual circumstances and needs.

Model Sentencing Act of the National Council on Crime and Delinquency, 1972

The Legislature finds and declares that the purpose of imprisonment for crime is punishment.

Section 1170 of the Penal Code of the State of California

During the last decade there has been a rather dramatic turnaround in the direction of thinking about crime as well as in the prevailing crime policy. This change has been characterized by an elevated public awareness of and concern about crime, the triumph of law-and-order rhetoric,[1] and a striking departure from previous assumptions about sentencing and punishment.[2] In all of its particulars, it has been a change from the formerly predominant liberal consensus, what might be called a soft view of crime, toward an as yet incomplete but nevertheless evident criminal justice realism, what might be called a hard view of crime.[3] Perhaps the clearest indication of both the direction and magnitude of this change is the broad rejection of rehabilitation as the guiding ideal in criminal sentencing and its replacement with notions of just deserts or incapacitation.[4]

For almost one hundred years rehabilitation was the predominant, though by no means exclusive, purpose upon which criminal sentencing was based. Its predominance was reflected in the widespread practice of indeterminacy in sentencing and the equally widespread use of parole. Indeterminacy in sentencing, the basis on which the rehabilitative ideal was brought into the everyday operations of the criminal courts, has three central elements. First, legislatures do not establish precise or fixed penalties for particular offenses. Instead they establish a broad range, or just a statutory minimum, within which sentences for particular offenders are to be assigned. Second, responsibility for fixing sentences is delegated to the judge, who exercises wide discretion in discharging that responsibility. Third, the sentence as pronounced by the judge does not determine the actual amount of time served by criminals who are incarcerated; that determination is left to parole boards, which make release decisions on the basis of evidence that prisoners have been successfully rehabilitated.

Beginning in the early 1970s, state after state began to reconsider each of the three elements of indeterminate sentencing. By the early 1980s more than thirty states had enacted mandatory minimum sentence laws for particularly serious crimes, and some states—like California and Minnesota—enacted comprehensive determinate sentencing legislation. Furthermore, almost twenty states had either abolished parole release for the majority of crimes and criminals or imposed guidelines to structure decisions on parole release.[5] A rather radical turnabout thus had occurred.

In their search for greater determinacy in sentencing the states have adopted different models.[6] But in each of these models the object is to establish clear and explicit standards, known or knowable in advance of any particular sentencing decision, which determine the nature and amount or duration of punishment appropriate for any offense.[7] Many states have adopted mandatory minimum sentences for particular offenses, ranging from New York's drug law enacted in 1973 to the Massachusetts gun law which imposes a one-year sentence of imprisonment for anyone convicted of carrying and possessing a firearm without a license or permit.[8] In addition, some statutory sentencing schemes attempt to be comprehensive in their coverage. They specify what are called presumptive sentences or sentence ranges and require judges to impose those sentences unless there are extraordinary aggravating or mitigating circumstances. Yet another type of determinate sentencing arrangement involves the promulgation of sentencing guidelines not by a state legislature but by an expert "sentencing commission." In some states such guidelines carry the force of law; in others, they are merely advisory.

No matter the form, all types of determinant sentencing represent an explicit rejection of the goals and philosophy of rehabilitation. The extent of the embrace of determinacy indicates the emergence of a new consensus on sentencing policy, a consensus that has moved us into a new era in the annals of American criminal justice.[9] The reasons for the development of this consensus as well as its political meaning remain largely unexamined. However, there is a philosophical and political logic to criminal sentencing which gives rise to particular tendencies and approaches. At a time when one set of tendencies and approaches is being dismantled and replaced by another, some attention to both philosophy and politics seems appropriate. It is my purpose to focus on the rejection of rehabilitation and to explore the philosophical premises behind the movement for determinacy.

The Rehabilitative Ideal

Rehabilitation has a long history as one of the major goals of criminal punishment. Its history arises from the application of utilitarianism to crime and can be traced at least as far back as the middle of the eighteenth century.[10] From its inception, the rehabilitative ideal has been closely allied with the goal of specific deterrence—the attempt to use sentencing to reduce the chance that those convicted of crime would, after punishment, engage in subsequent criminal conduct. Punishment in the rehabilitative ideal could simultaneously work for the improvement of individual criminals and effect a reduction in crime.[11]

Yet the achievements of rehabilitation have always been difficult to measure. Writing in the 1830s, Beaumont and Tocqueville observed that "theories on the reform of prisoners are vague and uncertain. It is not yet known to what degree the wicked may be regenerated and by what means this regeneration may be obtained."[12] This uncertainty did not translate into an abandonment of the ideal, at least until the most recent period. Indeed, throughout the late eighteenth and early nineteenth centuries substantial intellectual and political efforts were devoted to finding an effective program of rehabilitative punishment.[13]

The vehicle for such a program was first provided by the invention of the penitentiary.[14] As its name implies, the penitentiary was looked to as a refuge, an opportunity for criminals to reflect on their actions and to do penance so that they might assume a position of harmony with the laws of civil society. Richard Schwartz notes that as early as 1778 the British Parliament authorized the establishment of such a place of refuge, the purpose of which was to employ "sobriety, cleanliness and medical assistance, . . . a regular series of labor . . . solitary confinement during the intervals of work, and . . . religious instructions to preserve and amend the health of . . . offenders, to inure them to habits of industry, to guard them from pernicious company and to accustom them to serious reflection and to teach them both the principles and practice of every Christian moral duty."[15] Those sentiments expressed the hopes of American rehabilitationists as much as those of their British counterparts.

Imprisonment was looked to as a form of moderate punishment which Montesquieu, among others, had argued was most appropriate to a republican society; or as Foucault suggests, it was regarded as the "gentle way in punishment."[16] Imprisonment was, of course, only gentle by way of contrast with the systems of execution and torture that it superseded. The prison was regarded as a place for reflection on the moral character of criminal activity, a place where criminals could develop the strength of character to turn away from crime toward a respectable life. Prisoners were isolated from each other and from most other human contact, were deprived of most opportunities for work, and were expected to spend most of their time in solitary contemplation.[17] Reform or rehabilitation was seen as a process of clarification and control: clarifying the kind of life which the repenting prisoner wished to establish and exerting self-control. Rehabilitation required an act of will; imprisonment facilitated that act of will.

The modern rehabilitative ideal is a product not of the penitentiary movement of the eighteenth century but rather of the late nineteenth century. Rehabilitation as we know it became possible only with the emergence of social science and the professionalization of care. The emergence of "the science of man" made possible the full transformation of criminal punishment and its incorporation of the rehabilitative ideal such that it was possible to argue that "in its function the power to punish is not essentially different from that of curing or educating."[18] The crystallization of an understanding of human motivation and human behavior ushered in the dawn of the modern phase of rehabilitation—namely an acting upon criminals, a programming of their activities. Where once the path to reform was the path of solitude, the rehabilitative ideal in its modern version proposed observation, classification, organization, prescription, program, regimen, and work. The prisoner was to be the field of practice; science would substitute for religious conversion.

In order to understand the contemporary fate of the rehabilitative ideal, one must grasp its embeddedness in an entire social apparatus of control, supervision, and normalization. As Michel Foucault makes clear, the penitentiary and its emphasis on rehabilitation were part of a radical disruption and reconstitution of the organization of social life. In earlier periods, Foucault argues, "the order of the crime, the order of sin and the order of bad conduct remained separate." By the late nineteenth century, punishment had been incorporated into a disciplinary apparatus that organized and controlled the entire society. By that time, "as medicine, psychology, education, public assistance, 'social work' assumed an ever greater share of the powers of supervision and assessment, the penal apparatus . . . became medicalized, psychologized and educationalized."[19] Punishment and discipline became part of a single continuum, the success of the latter making it possible for the former to become more refined, more "gentle," more penetrating, and more active.

Yet the modern ideas and ideals of rehabilitation, dependent as they may have been on the new areas of knowledge Foucault cites, could not have taken hold (at least in the United States) without philosophical and political legitimacy for the activism that modern rehabilitation requires. A reconstitution of political theory was necessary to make way for new dimensions of state intervention in and regulation of the lives of criminals. This reconstitution was provided during the late nineteenth century by the ideas of Progressivism.[20]

Perhaps the key to Progressive ideas was the view that the state could and should be used as an instrument of social improvement. Rejecting the traditional liberal argument that state and society should be separated, the Progressives embraced a theory of state paternalism which encouraged state intervention to aid those who were unable to care for themselves adequately. Progressives were particularly attentive to the idea of human needs, and they were eager to identify deviation from norms of upper-middle-class life, to which the Progressives adhered, as indicative of neediness. This led to an exaggerated belief in the capacities of the state and in its benevolence. As David Rothman puts it, "the major tenet of Progressive thought was that only the state could make the individual free. Only the enlarged authority of the government could satisfy the particular needs of all the citizens." State action became the mode for bridging the gap between the rich and the poor, between the native and the immigrant, between the criminal and the law-abiding citizen, and for building a common culture. Progressives sought an enlarged role not only for the state but also for social science knowledge within their activist state. They were true believers in the capacity to know and understand social life and its causal mysteries. They embraced a rather new, and to them exciting, pragmatic positivism. They believed that social knowledge could and should be used in the service of social improvement.[21] Theirs was a special combination of moralism, intellectual enlightenment, and the seeds of modern liberal thought.

In the context of crime and criminal justice, the Progressive idea denied that there was an inevitable adversarial relationship between offender and the state.[22] Offenders were to be the object of the same state-sponsored efforts at improvement that were made available to aid immigrants and wayward children. Crime provided the occasion for yet another benevolent exercise of enlightened state power. Rehabilitation fit nicely into their program of social reform; it suggested that the marriage of state power and social knowledge would both reform the criminal and reduce crime.

While Progressivism did not invent the modern version of rehabilitation, it did provide it legitimacy. What is the content of the rehabilitative ideal that was so appealing to Progressives and so dominant for so long? The rehabilitative ideal has four central elements: a view of crime and its causes, a view of the proper relationship between the state and the accused, a view of the proper scope of state power and official authority, and a view of the proper disposition toward and design of criminal punishment. As Richard Schwartz sees it, the rehabilitative ideal: "means the purposeful reduction or elimination of an offender's subsequent criminal behavior through a program of planned intervention. This definition contains three elements all of which are necessary parts of the core concept of rehabilitation. The purpose of rehabilitation is to reduce subsequent crime; its program is a planned intervention to do so; and its effect is the actual reduction or elimination of criminality in the offender's behavior."[23]

Rehabilitative punishment assumes that criminal behavior reflects some personal defect which can be identified and altered.[24] At its extreme, this approach treats criminal conduct as if it were indicative of some pathology. Crime is regarded as a sickness; as such, crime carries no blameworthiness and is morally neutral. Criminals are regarded as victims rather than victimizers. Their acts should provoke neither anger nor vengeance. Instead, criminals need to be diagnosed and cured. As Herbert Morris describes the rehabilitative approach, "Actions diverging from some conception of the normal are viewed as manifestations of a disease in the way in which one might today regard the arm and leg movements of an epileptic during a seizure. . . . What a person does, then, is assimilated, on this concept, to what . . . a person undergoes. . . . [The] distinction between mere events or happenings and human actions is erased."[25]

Crime is, then, neither a random event nor a fully rational choice. It is caused. By locating the causes of crime within the individual, rehabilitation treats crime as if it were equivalent to a physical disease. And by assimilating crime and disease, rehabilitation makes way for a nonadversarial relationship between the "accused" and the state.[26] Rehabilitative punishment requires a medical approach in determining who needs treatment. In contrast with the fully adversarial, due-process approach to the criminal justice system, the medical approach stresses the essential compatibility of interests between the state and the accused. The alleged criminal has an interest in being helped, in being rid of his disease and its symptoms. The state has a similar interest in normalizing the criminal, but that normalization requires an accurate diagnosis. Unlike the emphasis of due process on procedural regularity and rule following, the medical approach stresses the need for flexibility and discretion.[27] Officials want to help the suspect, and as a result, the suspect does not need to be protected from them.[28]

Although a rehabilitative approach to sentencing may have entailed a medical orientation in the earlier stages of the criminal justice system, rehabilitation as a guiding goal for criminal punishment has, in fact, coexisted with a wide variety of approaches in the process of guilt determination. In many ways, individualization is the central concept of the rehabilitative theory. Since the causes of crime are located within the lives of particular offenders, and since the object is to cure offenders, the criminal rather than the crime is the particular focus of concern.[29] Rehabilitative punishment requires that the punishment, more accurately the treatment, be made to suit the offender and be responsive to his particular needs—not because of what he has done but because of some condition with which he is assumed to be afflicted. Emphasis is placed on present suffering and the hope for future recovery. As Herbert Morris suggests, rehabilitation seeks to "help and to benefit the individual who is suffering. . . . The individual suffering has not merited by his disease the good we seek to bestow upon him, but has, because he is a creature that has the capacity to feel pain, a claim upon our sympathies."[30]

Rehabilitation does not require limits and formal legal restraints because it is a benefit. Its boundaries and precise timing cannot be programmed because rehabilitative punishment is individualized and is oriented toward cure. Thus the linkage between rehabilitation and indeterminacy is forged. Final authority is lodged with experts trained in designing treatment programs and in recognizing when a cure has been effected. The conception of the criminal as violator of the social contract deserving swift, certain, and painful payback is replaced with a concept of the norm and with understanding of deviance. The deviant is to be remade. The state is to guard the social order through a system of diagnosis, prescription, confinement, and enforced treatment, all of which is justified in the name of social defense.

The Critique of Rehabilitation: Toward Determinacy in Sentencing

The decline of the rehabilitative ideal as the guiding philosophy of criminal punishment was brought about by a rather unusual coalition of political antagonists. Liberals and conservatives united in a common rejection of its adequacy and appropriateness.[31] Though their criticisms arose from very different starting points and were motivated by very different concerns, liberals and conservatives were able to unite in opposition to a philosophy which seemed to fail on its own terms and which both believed had lost its political appeal.

During the 1970s, when the coalition against rehabilitation was cemented, neither liberals nor conservatives wanted to be identified as indifferent to the crime problem. Though in recent decades liberals have viewed crime as more threatening as a political issue, conservatives, with their escalated law-and-order rhetoric, were caught in a situation where they seemed to promise more than they could produce. The high crime rate that prevailed during the 1970s and the corresponding elevation of anxiety about crime drove liberals and conservatives together—the former out of a fear that they would be blamed for the crime problem, the latter out of a desire to make good on their crime-fighting credentials. If neither could guarantee immediate and striking reductions in crime, liberals and conservatives both could appear tough by tightening up on overly lenient laws and advocating more swift and certain punishment.

While neither victimization nor the fear of crime was experienced by all groups (indeed, both are much more prevalent among people living in cities), fear of crime rose more rapidly during the 1960s and 1970s than did the experience of direct or personal victimization.[32] The fear of crime pushed crime itself into the forefront of electoral politics at the local, state, and national levels. Beginning in 1964, the law-and-order issue, as it was called, played a prominent part in campaign rhetoric.[33] The crime issue was placed on the national political agenda by Barry Goldwater and George Wallace, both of whom attacked President Johnson and the liberal Congress for fostering an atmosphere of permissiveness and for being soft on crime. They criticized the Supreme Court for its decisions in favor of criminal rights. In 1964 and in every presidential election since, the crime issue has been part of a larger complex of campaign themes aimed to exploit fear of rapid social change and of the so-called new morality and to advocate a retreat to conventional American values. As Senator Goldwater put it in accepting the 1964 Republican presidential nomination:

> Tonight there is violence in our streets, corruption in our highest offices, aimlessness among our youth, anxiety among our elderly, and there is virtual despair among the many who look beyond material success toward the inner meaning of their lives. . . . The growing menace in our country tonight, to personal safety, to life, to limb and to property, in homes, in churches, in the playgrounds and places of business, particularly in our great cities, is the mounting concern of every thoughtful citizen in the

> United States. Security from domestic violence, no less than foreign, is the most elementary and fundamental purpose of any government and a government that cannot fulfill this purpose is one that cannot long command the loyalty of its citizens.[34]

Such rhetoric also took as its object the problem of leniency in sentencing. Throughout the 1970s, politicians complained that too few criminals were being put in jail and that those incarcerated were not kept behind bars for long enough. This rhetoric was reflected in a growing punitiveness in public attitudes toward crime. For example, support for the death penalty increased from 47 percent in 1970 to 67 percent in 1980; similarly, there was a growth of over 15 percent (from 65 to 80 percent) in the number of people who believed that courts did not deal harshly enough with criminals. The 1970s were a time when politicians, employing the rhetoric of law and order, were able to "take advantage of punitive dispositions about crime that are rooted in American culture."[35]

Neither political rhetoric nor public opinion was specifically directed toward the rehabilitative ideal. The liberal/conservative coalition against rehabilitation was an outgrowth of a loss of faith among academic criminologists, many of whom had been proponents or advocates of rehabilitation.[36] There was, and is, a wide range of views among those criminologists—ranging from retributivists, who see in rehabilitation a denial of the requisites of substantive justice, to utilitarians, who reject rehabilitation because of its failure to prevent recidivism, to rights-oriented liberals, who reject rehabilitation as part of a broader program designed to protect the procedural rights of suspects and those convicted of crime.

The Retributivist Critique

The retributivist critique of rehabilitation is represented in this volume in the essays by Walter Berns and Daniel Robinson. While they disagree in many fundamental and important ways, both reject rehabilitation because it is overly concerned with the needs of the offender and too little concerned with expressing moral outrage at the act of crime itself. Both see rehabilitative punishment as the product of an undeserved faith in social science and an unwillingness to label evil things as evil.

Berns and Robinson part company on the question of the justification for a retributivist system of punishment. While both begin with the idea that such a system would embody and express justice, Berns suggests that retribution is an appropriate basis for punishment since it comports with the views and feelings of "the typical citizen" and, in so doing, is responsive to the legitimate anger which crime evokes in such citizens. Berns seeks to legitimate the expression of anger and to suggest the inappropriateness of compassion. For him, compassion is a misguided and "easy" response to crime, a response reflecting the confusion of intellectuals. Retribution rejects such inappropriate compassion and responds to and satisfies the justifiable anger of the just person.[37] In so doing, retributive punishment promotes "law abidingness," helps to "preserve free government" and "the moral community."[38]

Robinson's commitment to retributive punishment is founded in his belief that it alone meets the demands of justice. For him, Berns's utilitarian defense of retribution is both unnecessary and dangerous—unnecessary because justice alone should be the object of the law, dangerous because it would hold justice hostage to majority sentiment. Robinson rejects rehabilitation by implication because it offends "principle," denies moral autonomy, and invites and encourages an insidious determinism, which in turn weakens our will and capacity to engage in moral action. Justice, Robinson argues, requires human beings to rise above the very conditions that rehabilitative approaches look to as providing exculpations from blame. Whereas Berns is willing to bow in the direction of the historicity of criminal justice policy and to acknowledge its relevance in the life of the polity, Robinson's defense of retribution is at war with history and context. A just system of criminal punishment knows no history or context.

Another important and powerful retributive critique of rehabilitation is contained in an essay by Herbert Morris. Like Robinson, Morris argues that rehabilitative punishment is based upon and embodies a corrosive determinism. According to Morris, a proper system of punishment is one which maximizes individual freedom of choice. In rehabilitative systems, "the individual's free choice ceases to be the determinative factor in how others respond to him . . . how we respond in [such a] . . . system . . . is not conditioned upon what he has chosen but rather on what symptoms he has manifested or may manifest and what the best therapy for the disease is."[39] By denying that crime is a product of human choice, rehabilitative punishment diminishes—indeed threatens—our dignity as human beings.

This denial of dignity occurs in a rehabilitative system, Morris argues, because our choices aren't taken seriously. Actions are reduced to events. We are asked to depend on the compassion of others and to break the linkage between what we do and what we get. The rehabilitative approach wars against a culture of achievement and diminishes the satisfaction we get from leading a life in which we make ourselves by what we do. For Morris, rehabilitation drains human life of energy and purpose by displaying a lack of respect for "the moral status of individuals."[40]

Morris advocates a system of punishment which takes choices seriously and metes out punishment on the basis of what persons do. Rehabilitation is unacceptable because, in the final analysis, it denies criminals their right to be punished. In its attempt to substitute compassion for judgment, rehabilitation deprives humans of that which is most essentially human. In arguing for the right of criminals to be punished on the basis of what their acts deserve, Morris distinguishes between the guilt engendered by a wrongful choice and the shame associated with being sick. The former is preferable, he suggests, because "there are relatively simple ways of ridding ourselves of the feeling we have, that is, gaining forgiveness or taking the punishment, but with shame we have to bear it until we no longer are the person who has behaved in the shameful way."[41]

The retributivist critique relies upon an argument about substantive moral principles. It speaks the language of justice and is relatively clear about what justice entails. Justice is not, in this concept, satisfied by procedure; it requires that the guilty be punished. They should suffer in proportion to the suffering they have inflicted. Retributivists invoke a universalized conception of human dignity and in so doing advance a critique of the therapeutic orientation of rehabilitation. At the heart of this argument is an attack on social science knowledge, a wish to depart from the relativism and the determinism implicit in the paradigmatic understanding of crime.

The Utilitarian Critique

While the retributivist wishes to reconnect punishment and justice, the utilitarian wishes to make punishment an efficacious response to an escalating crime rate.[42] The utilitarian critique points to the rather impressive evidence that rehabilitative punishment does not work, that prisoners who are treated through various rehabilitative programs display high recidivism rates, and that there is no reliable technology for rehabilitation.[43] Utilitarians reject rehabilitation because of its failure to advance the goal of crime control adequately. For them, crime is not just an issue of justice; it is itself a deep social disorder, a threat to the social fabric. For utilitarians the escalating crime rate of the 1960s and 1970s posed a threat to the "maintenance of meaningful human communities."[44]

Perhaps the clearest statement of the utilitarian view is found in the work of James Wilson. Wilson's book *Thinking about Crime* helped to pave the way for policymakers intent on getting beyond rehabilitation. Like the retributivists, Wilson attacks what he sees as the prevailing social science orthodoxy which yoked punishment policy (rehabilitation) to social policy (welfarism) as the only "morally defensible and substantively efficacious strategy for reducing crime."[45] Wilson recognizes that proponents of rehabilitation did not believe that it alone could rid society of the crime problem. Crime was, in the liberal view, a product of poverty and deprivation; thus, steps had to be taken to deal with those causes before rehabilitation could be effective.

Wilson's work is marked by a profound skepticism that we can understand enough about the causes of crime to do anything effective about it. Root causes, according to Wilson, are unfathomable and unknowable. Crime is endemic to organized social life. One should not expect to eradicate crime or to design social programs that can eliminate it. Wilson argues that there is no reliable evidence of any connection between government expenditures on or efforts at social welfare and reduction in the crime rate. He observes, to the contrary, that "crime rates have increased during the very period (1963–70) when there were great advances in the income, schooling and housing of almost all segments of the society." Thus the Great Society was a great failure as a crime control or reduction policy.

Wilson criticizes the rehabilitative ideal for its understanding of the nature of crime. Crime should not be viewed as a sickness; the criminal should not be seen as a victim. Crime results from a cost/benefit calculus. Crime policy should be directed at altering the costs and benefits associated with criminal behavior:

> Criminals may be willing to run greater risks (or they may have a weaker code of morality) that the average citizen, but if the expected cost of crime

> goes up without a corresponding increase in the expected benefits, then the would-be criminal—unless he or she is among that small fraction of criminals who are utterly irrational—engages in less crime, just as the average citizen will be less likely to take a job as a day laborer if the earnings from this occupation, relative to those from other occupations, goes down.[46]

Wilson argues that there is no easy way to alter cost/benefit calculations, but it is naive to believe (as do advocates of rehabilitation) that the nature of criminal behavior can be altered by changing the criminal.

Wilson embraces unqualifiedly the view that rehabilitation has failed. He cites empirical evidence to support this conclusion, but beyond evidence lies a matter of logic which should undermine faith in rehabilitation.

> It requires not merely optimistic but heroic assumptions about the nature of man to lead one to suppose that a person, finally sentenced after (in most cases) many brushes with the law, and having devoted a good part of his youth and young adulthood to misbehavior of every sort, should by either the solemnity of prison or the skillfulness of a counselor, come to see the error of his ways and to experience a transformation of his character. . . . Criminal rehabilitation requires producing . . . changes in unwilling subjects under conditions of duress or indifference.[47]

Once we recognize that rehabilitation cannot work, we can develop a crime policy based on "a sober view of man and his institutions that would permit reasonable things to be accomplished, foolish things abandoned and utopian things forgotten."[48]

The utilitarian critique suggests that one reasonable step would be to increase the severity of punishments. Rehabilitation puts too few people in jail for too little time. Yet Wilson recognizes that increased severity in and of itself will not deter crime; indeed, it might prove counterproductive. Penalties must be structured which are severe enough to impose substantial costs but not so severe as to inhibit those charged with administering criminal justice from actually imposing them. Nor can one expect, Wilson argues, that even if they were carried out such penalties would have much impact. For him it is the certainty of arrest and conviction which is crucial. Here Wilson parts company with other utilitarians who seem to believe in the independent value of increased severity.[49]

What is most troubling to Wilson is that at least until the mid-1970s, in the name of rehabilitation we had been moving away from isolation and incapacitation. Probation and decarceration, as well as community-based corrections, operated to keep the criminal in the community and in so doing had the effect of further exacerbating the destructive effect of crime on the cohesion of social relations in American cities. No matter what the effects of imprisonment are on potential criminals or on deterring those incarcerated from committing crimes in the future—effects about which Wilson is very skeptical—Wilson believes that the benefit to be derived from isolation is clear and obvious: whatever criminals may do "when they are released, they cannot harm society while confined or closely supervised."[50]

We should punish those who commit crimes because they have done wrong, but the decision as to how to punish should be guided by the efficacy of punishment in preventing crime. Isolation and incapacitation, Wilson believes, would produce major gains in crime reduction. Penalties should be tailored to fit the crime, and rehabilitation should be abandoned. Abandonment of the rehabilitative ideal would, in Wilson's view, allow for the implementation of a modest, realistic, and effective sentencing policy.

The utilitarian critique appeals to "realism" and focuses almost exclusively on reduction of crime. Instead of an abstract concern for substantive justice, the day-to-day impact of crime would guide sentencing. Moreover, utilitarians link the failures of rehabilitation with the alleged failures and excesses of the welfare state.[51] This provided a powerful and attractive political symbol in the decade of the 1970s and enabled legislators to portray themselves as cutting wasteful and ineffective government expenditures while strengthening the capacity of the state to cope with crime by supporting both cuts in welfare spending and measures to end indeterminacy in criminal sentencing.

The utilitarian critique of rehabilitation thus was part of a general drift to the right in American politics during the late 1970s. Yet it was ultimately the abandonment of rehabilitation by rights-oriented liberals that furthered the movement toward greater determinacy in criminal sentencing.

The Liberal Critique

Since rehabilitation had been a primary stepchild of twentieth-century liberalism, the liberal critique of rehabilitation meant the withdrawal of its traditional last line of defense.[52] The retributionists' major concern is the failure of rehabilitation to fulfill the requirements of substantive justice, and the central element of the utilitarian critique is a concern with crime reduction. In contrast, the liberal critique focuses on the rights of suspects, criminals, and prisoners. The rehabilitative ideal came under criticism from the liberal left because of the price it exacted from those subject to its regimen and because of its failure adequately to protect individual rights and to guard against gross abuses.[53]

The liberal critique was part of a broad effort in the 1960s to expand the rights of criminal suspects. That decade saw a dramatic movement from crime control toward enlarged due process as the guide for the processing of criminal suspects.[54] Liberal expansion of criminal rights served first and foremost to limit the discretionary power of police and prosecutors. This expansion was moved by a concern to minimize the chance of error in the adjudication of criminal guilt. Discretionary decisions were viewed as entrusting too much power to officials whose interests were not in the protection of rights but instead were concentrated on rapid processing and on conviction rates. Moreover, emphasis on the rights of criminal suspects expressed a belief in equality, in balancing the contest between the state and the accused. Guarantees of the right to counsel, for example, were designed to provide countervailing access to legal advice for criminal defendants. A fair process both limited discretion and guaranteed equality.

By the end of the 1960s the liberal agenda for criminal rights had become the law of the land. The rehabilitative ideal coexisted side by side with an almost fully realized due process from arrest to conviction. This coexistence was one which could not long escape notice. Virtually unlimited discretion in sentencing seemed incompatible with a program designed to limit discretion in guilt determination. A highly individualized sentencing system seemed incompatible with a commitment to equal justice under law. The most important and influential recognition of these tensions was contained in Marvin Frankel's *Criminal Sentences,* the liberal equivalent of Wilson's *Thinking about Crime.* In his book Frankel presents a thorough and comprehensive attack on rehabilitation. In his view, it is based upon a false understanding of the nature of crime: the assumption that criminals are sick and in need of treatment. Most criminals, Frankel argues, are neither in need of nor responsive to programs of treatment. Like his utilitarian allies, Frankel is persuaded that rehabilitation doesn't work, that it is rather silly to expect prisons to remake human character.

Yet what is central to Frankel is not the utility of rehabilitative sentencing. Frankel's indictment of the rehabilitative ideal focuses instead on two problems—discretion and disparity. By giving judges so much discretion, rehabilitation sentencing creates a sentencing system that is, in effect, lawless. Judicial discretion is an inevitable part of a system in which legislatures set broad sentencing ranges for each offense and provide no standards for locating particular cases within the prescribed range. Judges are left on their own to decide who gets what punishment for what offense. This, Frankel suggests, is incompatible with our commitment to the rule of law and the protection of individual rights. In the name of rehabilitation and individualized justice, indeterminacy allows sentencing to be guided by "the wide spectrum of character, neuroses and daily vagary encountered among occupants of the trial bench."[55]

According to Frankel, discretion, individualized justice, and indeterminacy result in grossly unequal sentences and in gross disparities in actual time served among criminals committing similar offenses. Reliance on parole boards to determine actual time served further compounds the problem. There is great inconsistency, he suggests, in the sentencing patterns of individual judges and even greater inconsistency when one examines sentencing across judges. Widespread judicial discretion necessarily must result in widely divergent criminal sentences:

> The evidence is conclusive that judges of widely varying attitudes on sentencing, administering statutes that confer huge measures of discretion, mete out widely divergent sentences where the divergences are explainable only by the variations among the judges, not by material differences in the defendants or their crimes. . . . What would require proof of a weighty kind and something astonishing in the way of theoretical explanations would be the suggestion that assorted judges subject to little more than their own unfettered wills could be expected to impose consistent sentences.[56]

Not only is it impossible to know in advance what kind of sentence a crime may engender, it is equally difficult to know, even after imprisonment, how long one will be incarcerated. Disparity in criminal punishment is incompatible with the promise of equal protection of the law, and such disparity indicates that a sentencing system committed to treatment has degenerated into a system which is arbitrary and capricious.[57]

Frankel's response was to recommend steps to limit judicial discretion, thereby introducing greater determinacy into the sentencing process. He suggested that legislatures should provide a clear statement of the purposes a community wishes to pursue in the application of criminal punishment. In addition, legislatures might codify the factors to be considered in sentencing and "prescribe guidelines for the application and assessment of those factors."[58] This combination of reforms would move away from the gross abuses of the rehabilitative ideal and toward a situation in which sentences would be "stated with maximum certainty, based almost entirely on factors known on the day of sentencing, and determined with the nearest approach we can make to objective, equal and 'impersonal' evaluation of the relevant qualities of both the criminal and the crime."[59]

Liberal criticisms of rehabilitation do not focus exclusively on the values of predictability and equal treatment; they are equally concerned with the effect of rehabilitative punishment on prisoners. Some see in the rehabilitative ideal a justification for a kind of therapeutic fascism within prisons. Rehabilitation allows prisoners to be coerced, manipulated, and subjected to humiliating rituals whose object is to please prison officials and convince parole boards that the inmate is ready to return to civilized life. Rehabilitative punishment turns inmates into con artists whose skill at manipulating appearances counts as much as their willingness to internalize conventional norms. Liberal critics see rehabilitation as a social control device within the prison. As Jessica Mitford argues, " 'individualized treatment' is primarily a device for breaking the convict's will to resist and hounding him into compliance with institutional demands and is thus a means of exerting maximum control over the convict population."[60] Rehabilitation also was used to justify abuses of the privacy and dignity of prisoners, as well as justifying longer incarceration than the sentencing judge would have prescribed in many cases.[61]

As liberals became clearer about the need to protect the rights of prisoners and active in litigating conditions in prisons, the rehabilitative ideal itself became the focus of criticism. Liberal advocates of prisoners' rights portrayed rehabilitation as an excuse for taking advantage of the vulnerability of prisoners. Here benevolence became its opposite. In the captive environs of the prison the rehabilitative program further weakened prisoners and increased their dependency and frustration.

The liberal critique found its most complete expression in the mid-

1970s with the publication of *Doing Justice*, the Report of the Committee for the Study of Incarceration, a committee brought together by the Field Foundation to consider the future of imprisonment. This committee began by endorsing the view that "despite every effort and every attempt, correctional treatment programs have failed" and that rehabilitative approaches had, in practice, been "cruel and punitive."[62] It suggested that the good-faith effort which is necessarily part of the rehabilitative ideal allowed people of conscience to tell themselves that what they were doing in the name of treatment and help was justified, even if its practice seemed to violate basic standards of fairness and to jeopardize individual rights. Like Marvin Frankel, the committee opposed the wide latitude accorded to judges and parole boards in the rehabilitative approach. The committee joined with Frankel in condemning disparity and unpredictability and noted that due process of law required greater uniformity and certainty than the rehabilitative ideal could provide.

In place of rehabilitation, the committee proposed that "just deserts" should be the philosophy guiding criminal sentencing. The committee rejected retribution because retribution portrays punishment as a mere "requital-of-evil." This rather straightforward reciprocity, it argued, was insufficient. Just deserts, in contrast, directs attention to the moral quality of conduct:

> Someone who infringes the rights of others . . . does wrong and deserves blame for his conduct. It is because he deserves blame that the sanctioning authority is entitled to choose a response that expresses moral disapproval: namely, punishment. In other words, the sanction ought not only to deprive the offender of the "advantage" obtained by his disregard of the rules . . . , but also in a manner that ascribes blame. . . . Blaming persons who commit wrongful acts is . . . a way of reaffirming the moral values that were "infringed."[63]

While the liberal position resembles the retributivist in its emphasis on the moral quality of the act as the basis of punishment, retributivists are typically impatient with the concern for the rights of suspects which is so central to the liberal argument. Whereas retributivists are prepared to deemphasize process values to achieve punishment objectives, liberals—even as they embrace just deserts—attempt to reassert the process rights of persons accused of crime. Their embrace of just deserts grows out of an interest in the process of punishment and a belief in the inseparability of process rights and substantive justice.

Doing Justice advocates a system of presumptive sentences. Such a system has the advantage of reducing discretion, thereby increasing certainty and predictability as well as insuring that "uniform treatment is provided for the unexceptional cases that make up the bulk of judges' caseloads, while still allowing variation in out-of-the-ordinary cases."[64] Finally, *Doing Justice* argues that sentences should, on the average, be reduced in length, and that sentences and time served under a rehabilitative sentencing system often are disproportionate to the seriousness of the offense.

Doing Justice articulated an agenda of reform which connected the goals of protecting individual rights and reducing sentencing disparity. This, in combination with the critique of imprisonment, provided liberals with a politically attractive position on the crime issue, a basis to cooperate with retributivists and utilitarians, and yet space within which to maintain a discrete position in discussions of crime and criminal justice policy.

Conclusion

Retributivists, utilitarians, and liberals were able to form a broad coalition against indeterminacy in sentencing. This coalition, in turn, provided a basis for political action without the need for new expenditures of funds or promises of dramatic reductions in the crime rate. A high crime rate and elevated public concern about crime provided the permissive conditions necessary to allow for the translation of the various critiques of rehabilitation into new sentencing policy. Getting beyond rehabilitation by ending indeterminacy has provided politicians with a way of responding to the crime problem and of satisfying a broad coalition of informed opinion.

While the effort to get beyond rehabilitation is far from complete, it appears to have a secure future. The broad coalition remains intact, and as yet there is no serious academic revisionism. There is, however, some evidence that utilitarian hopes that determinate sentencing would lead to greater punitiveness have not been realized. In most states where such schemes are now in effect there has not been a significant growth in the number of those committing serious crimes who receive incarcerative sentences, and there have been only marginal increases in the average length of sentences.[65] Determinate sentencing has, however, increased penalties for less serious offenses while leaving most of the dispositional patterns and practices established under indeterminate sentencing virtually unchanged.[66] Once again we see the extraordinary difficulty of anticipating the effect of reforms in criminal justice. Yet in spite of this difficulty, the movement to get beyond rehabilitation is likely to continue since so much of its support is not based on utilitarism considerations and there seems no more promising direction for change.

Notes

1. Stuart A. Scheingold, *The Politics of Law and Order: Street Crime and Public Policy* (New York: Longman, 1984).
2. Francis A. Allen, *The Decline of the Rehabilitative Ideal* (New Haven: Yale University Press, 1981).
3. Alfred Blumstein et al., *Research on Sentencing: The Search for Reform* (Washington, D.C.: National Academy Press, 1983).
4. See Norval Morris, *The Future of Imprisonment* (Chicago: University of Chicago Press, 1974); Stephen Clarke, "Determinate Sentencing," in *Encyclopedia of Crime and Justice*, ed. Sanford Kadish (New York: Free Press, 1983).
5. Jacqueline Cohen and Michael Tonry, "Sentencing Reforms and Their Impacts," in Blumstein, *Research on Sentencing*, p. 305.
6. See Andrew von Hirsch and Kathleen Hanrahan, "Determinate Penalty Systems in America," *Crime and Delinquency* 27 (1981): 289.
7. Clarke, "Determinate Sentencing," p. 1440.
8. Malcolm Feeley and Austin Sarat, *The Policy Dilemma: Federal Crime Policy and the Law Enforcement Assistance Administration, 1969–1978* (Minneapolis: University of Minnesota Press, 1980).
9. Franklin Zimring, "Sentencing Reform in the States," in *Reform and Punishment*, ed. Michael Tonry and Franklin Zimring (Chicago: University of Chicago Press, 1983).
10. Cesare Beccaria, *On Crimes and Punishment*, trans. Henry Paolucci (Indianapolis: Bobbs-Merrill, 1963; originally published in 1764).
11. Karl Menninger, *The Crime of Punishment* (New York: Viking Press, 1968).
12. Gustave de Beaumont and Alexis de Tocqueville, *On the Penitentiary System in the United States and Its Application to France*, trans. Francis Lieber (Carbondale: Southern Illinois University Press, 1964).
13. Richard Schwartz, "Rehabilitation," in Kadish, *Encyclopedia of Crime and Justice*.

14. David Rothman, *The Discovery of the Asylum* (Boston: Little, Brown, 1971).

15. Schwartz, "Rehabilitation," p. 136.

16. Michel Foucault, *Discipline and Punish* (New York: Vintage Books, 1979), p. 104.

17. Rothman, *Discovery of the Asylum.*

18. Foucault, *Discipline and Punish,* esp. p. 303.

19. Ibid., pp. 298–99, 306.

20. David Rothman, *Conscience and Convenience* (Boston: Little, Brown, 1980).

21. David Rothman, "The State as Parent," in *Doing Good,* ed. Willard Gaylin (New York: Pantheon, 1978), pp. 74, 75.

22. John Griffiths, "Ideology in Criminal Procedure," *Yale Law Journal* 79 (1970): 359.

23. Schwartz, "Rehabilitation," p. 136.

24. Menninger, *Crime of Punishment.*

25. Herbert Morris, "Persons and Punishment," in *Human Rights,* ed. Abraham Meldrew (Belmont, Calif.: Wadsworth, 1970), p. 116.

26. Griffiths, "Ideology in Criminal Procedure."

27. Allen, *Decline of the Rehabilitative Ideal.*

28. Menninger, *Crime of Punishment.*

29. Marvin Frankel, *Criminal Sentences* (New York: Hill and Wang, 1972).

30. Morris, "Persons and Punishment," p. 118.

31. See Zimring, "Sentencing Reform."

32. Wesley Skogan and Michael Maxfield, *Coping with Crime: Individual and Neighborhood Reactions* (Beverly Hills: Sage, 1981).

33. Feeley and Sarat, *The Policy Dilemma.*

34. Quoted in Richard Scammon and Ben Wattenberg, *The Real Majority* (New York: Coward, McCann, 1970), p. 37.

35. Scheingold, *The Politics of Law and Order,* pp. 47, 54.

36. Zimring, "Sentencing Reform."

37. Susan Jacoby, *Wild Justice* (New York: Harper & Row, 1983).

38. Walter Berns, "Retribution as the Ground for Punishment," in this volume.

39. Morris, "Persons and Punishment," p. 120.

40. Ibid., p. 122.

41. Ibid., p. 124.

42. Lynn Curtis, "The Conservative New Criminology," *Society* 17 (1977): 8.

43. Madelin Fleming, *Of Crimes and Rights* (New York: W. W. Norton, 1978); David

Greenberg, "The Correctional Effects of Corrections," in *Corrections and Punishments,* ed. David Greenberg (Beverly Hills: Sage, 1977); Andrew Hopkins, "Imprisonment and Recidivism," *Journal of Research in Crime and Delinquency* 13 (1976):13; Douglas Lipton et al., *The Effectiveness of Correctional Treatment* (New York: Praeger, 1975); Robert Martinson, "What Works?" *Public Interest* 35 (1974): 22; Pierce O'Donnell et al., *Toward a Just and Effective Sentencing System* (New York: Praeger, 1977).

44. James Wilson, *Thinking about Crime* (New York: Basic Books, 1975), p. 22.

45. Ibid., chap. 3.

46. Ibid., pp. 175–76.

47. Ibid., p. 170.

48. Ibid.

49. Ernest Van den Haag, *Punishing Criminals* (New York: Basic Books, 1975), chap. 3.

50. Wilson, *Thinking about Crime,* p. 173.

51. Fleming, *Of Crimes and Rights.*

52. Susan Martin, "The Politics of Sentencing Reform," in Blumstein, *Research on Sentencing,* p. 265.

53. Jessica Mitford, *Kind and Usual Punishment* (New York: Vintage Books, 1974).

54. Herbert Packer, *The Limits of the Criminal Sanction* (Stanford: Stanford University Press, 1968).

55. Frankel, *Criminal Sentences,* pp. 7, 21.

56. Ibid., p. 21.

57. John Coffee, "The Future of Sentencing Reform: Emerging Legal Issues in the Individualization of Justice," *Michigan Law Review* 73 (1975): 1361.

58. Frankel, *Criminal Sentences,* p. 103.

59. Ibid., pp. 101–2.

60. Mitford, *Kind and Usual Punishment,* p. 128.

61. Steven Schulhoffer, "Due Process of Sentencing," *University of Pennsylvania Law Review* 128 (1980): 733.

62. Andrew von Hirsch, *Doing Justice* (New York: Hill and Wang, 1976), p. xxxviii.

63. Ibid., pp. 48–49.

64. Ibid., p. 99.

65. Cohen and Tonry, "Sentencing Reforms"; Colin Lofton et al., "Mandatory Sentencing and Firearms Violence," *Law and Society Review* 17 (1983): 287.

66. Malcolm Feeley, *Court Reform on Trial* (New York: Basic Books, 1983).

Contributors

WALTER BERNS is John M. Olin University Professor in the department of government at Georgetown University. Former professor of political science at Cornell University and the University of Toronto, he is the author of *Freedom, Virtue, and the First Amendment*.

WILLIAM J. KUNKLE, JR., was First Assistant State's Attorney for Cook County, Illinois. A graduate of Northwestern University School of Law, he was chief prosecutor in the case of mass murderer John Wayne Gacy. Mr. Kunkle is now with Phelan, Pope and John, Ltd., of Chicago.

DANIEL N. ROBINSON is professor of psychology and chairman of the department at Georgetown University. He is the author of *Psychology and Law: Can Justice Survive the Social Sciences?* and *Toward a Science of Human Nature: Essays on the Psychologies of Hegel, Mill, Wundt, and James*.

AUSTIN D. SARAT is William Nelson Cromwell Professor of jurisprudence and political science at Amherst College. He is the author of *The Rule of Law and the American Legal System*.

JEFFREY LEIGH SEDGWICK is associate professor of political science at the University of Massachusetts, Amherst. He is the author of *Law Enforcement Planning: The Limits of Economic Analysis* and *Deterring Criminals: Policymaking in the American Political Tradition*.

JEROME H. SKOLNICK is professor of law (jurisprudence and social policy) at the University of California, Berkeley. He is the author of *Justice Without Trial,* and, most recently, coauthor with David H. Bayley of *The New Blue Line.*

FRED E. BAUMANN is former Director of the Public Affairs Conference Center and assistant professor of political science at Kenyon College.

KENNETH M. JENSEN is a former faculty member at Kenyon College and publications consultant to the Public Affairs Conference Center. He is currently director of research and studies at the United States Institute of Peace.

Author Index

Abrahamse, Allan, 96
Andenaes, Johannes, 4
Aristotle, 26, 30, 42, 44, 46, 50–60
Austin, J., 95

Beccaria, Cesare, 2–3, 6, 12
Bentham, Jeremy, 22, 24, 26
Brennan, William, 5
Brisbon, Henry, 65
Brockway, Zebulan, 103
Burger, Warren, 88

Chaiken, Jan, 98
Chaiken, Marcia, 98
Clark, Tom, 82
Cleaver, Eldridge, 63
Comte, Auguste, 22

Draco, 15–16, 33

Fogel, David, 72
Forst, Martin, 91
Foucault, Michel, 106–7
Frank, Phillip, 22
Frankel, Marvin, 89–90, 118–21
Frankfurter, Felix, 85
Freud, Sigmund, 10

Gacy, John, 65, 77
Goldwater, Barry, 111
Greenwood, Peter W., 96, 98

Hart, H. L. A., 1, 3, 82–83
Hempel, Carl, 30
Heracleitus, 17
Hesiod, 16
Hinckley, John, 78–79
Hobbes, Thomas, 9, 10
Hume, David, 22, 24, 31, 40

Jacobs, James, 93–94
Johnson, Lyndon B., 111

Kamisar, Yale, 88
Kant, Immanuel, viii, 1–3, 21, 23, 26, 42–50, 59–60
Kennedy, John F., 10
King, Martin Luther, 10
Krisberg, B., 95
Krojick, Kevin, 94

Lewis, C. S., 6
Locke, John, 28

Mach, Ernst, 22
Madison, James, 10
Mailer, Norman, 63
Manson, Charles, 10
Marshall, Thurgood, 3, 9
Marx, Karl, 27–28
Menninger, Karl, 5, 7, 63, 66
Mill, John Stuart, 19, 22, 24
Mitford, Jessica, 120
Montesquieu, baron de La Brède et de, 106
Morris, Herbert, 110, 113–14
Morris, Norval, 7, 62

Nagel, Thomas, 82
Neurath, Otto, 22
Nietzsche, Friedrich, vii, ix

Orwin, Clifford, 11, 12
Oswald, Lee Harvey, 10

Packer, Herbert L., viii, 12
Pakter, Walter, 88
Piaget, Jean, 24
Plato, 16, 42–44, 51, 55, 66

Rawls, John, 25
Rehnquist, William, 85
Rockefeller, Nelson, 4, 11

Rothman, David, 108
Rousseau, Jean Jacques, 12, 43

Saint-Simon, Henri, comte de, 22
Schlick, Moritz, 22
Schwartz, Richard, 106, 108
Silberman, Charles E., 63
Skinner, B. F., 31
Smith, Adam, 8–9
Socrates, 42
Solon, 15–16, 33
Speck, Richard, 10, 77
Stewart, Potter, 86

Tate, Sharon, 10
Thompson, James, 72
Tocqueville, Alexis de, 105–6

von Hirsch, Andrew, 89, 91

Wallace, George, 111
Wicker, Tom, 4–5, 7, 8, 11–12, 63
Wilkey, Malcolm, 88
Williams, Bernard, 82
Wilson, James Q., 64, 115–18
Wittgenstein, Ludwig, 22
Wolfgang, Marvin, 64

Subject Index

Abortion, 33–35
American Friends Service Committee, 4
American Law Institute, 5
Anger, 9–12, 21, 41–42, 57–60, 89, 109, 113
Autonomy. *See* Morals, and individual autonomy

Capital punishment, 66, 68, 75, 112
Committee for the Study of Incarceration, 7–8, 121
Compassion, for defendants, 10–12, 79, 113, 114
Constitution, U.S., 3, 23, 92, 94. *See also* individual Amendments
Crime rates, 67–68, 81, 98, 111, 115
Criminal rights. *See* Rights of suspects and prisoners

Deception, by law enforcement agents, 84–89
Descriptivism, 31–33, 40
Determinism, 16–19, 32, 113, 114
Deterrence, 2, 6, 62, 66–69, 81, 87, 105
Doing Justice, 7, 121–22

Eighth Amendment, 3, 92, 93
English law, 37
Equality of sexes, 34–36
Ethics. *See* Morals
Exclusionary rule, 73, 76–77, 84, 86–89

First Amendment, 34
First principles, 26, 28, 29, 39–40, 58–59
Fourth Amendment, 77
Friendship, as Aristotelian virtue, 55, 57, 59–60

Gay rights, 34–36
Greek society (ancient), 15–17, 22

Hedonism, 17–18, 50, 52

Insanity defense, 73, 77–79
Integrity of criminal justice system, 74–77, 82–99
Intent, criminal, 44, 56, 78–79, 85

Liberalism, 49, 63, 103–4, 108, 110–12, 115, 117–22

Mandatory sentences. *See* Sentencing
Media commentary on crime, 4–5, 11, 75, 78, 90
Model Penal Code, 5
Model Sentencing Act, 6–8, 103
Morals: as basis for justice, 15–40, 121; emotive theory of, 19–20, 22; and individual autonomy, 16–18, 25–26, 36, 39, 113; Kant's metaphysics of, 42–50; relativism and, 15, 21–29, 38–39, 54, 82, 114
Moral science, 28–40

National Institute on Crime and Delinquency, 5
Natural rights, 15, 25–27
New York Times, 4, 11

Parole, 32, 72, 91, 104, 120
Pathological model of criminality, 109–10, 113, 115, 118
Pluralistic society, 23, 27, 29
Positivism, 22–23
Preventive detention, 69–72
Prisoners' rights. *See* Rights of suspects and prisoners
Prisons: conditions in, 92–96, 120; invention of, 106–7; population figures for, 6, 94–95; uprisings in, 4–5, 11; violence in, 93–95
Progressivism, 106–8

Race, as factor in punishment, 33, 38–39, 97
Recidivism, 63–64, 71
Rehabilitation, 6–7, 41, 62, 64–66, 72, 81, 98, 104–23
Relativism. *See* Morals, relativism and
Responsibility, individual, 9, 25, 33, 36–37, 53–54, 59
Retribution, 1–12, 41–42, 58–60, 62, 73–76, 81–99, 112–15, 121–22
Rights of suspects and prisoners, 63, 74, 77, 86, 89, 111, 118, 120–21. *See also* Exclusionary rule, individual Amendments
Roman law (ancient), 21, 37

Selective incapacitation, 96–98
Sentencing, 6–8, 32, 62, 64, 71–76, 81, 84, 90–92, 98, 104–5, 109, 112, 117–23
Social sciences, 3, 7, 24, 29–39, 79, 106–7, 114–15
Socratic philosophers, 16–17
Stateville (Ill.) penitentiary, 93–95
Supreme Court decisions, U.S., 3, 5, 33–34, 63, 77, 85–87, 95, 111

Telishment, 25, 29
Thymos (spiritedness), 42, 58
Traynor, Roger J., 87

Utilitarianism, 2, 22–27, 50, 83–86, 96, 105, 112, 114–18, 122–23

Vengeance, 3, 9, 41, 73–74, 82, 109. *See also* Anger
Vienna Circle, 22